THE MOUNTAINS OF IRELAND

Errigal rising above Dunlewy in north-west Donegal

THE MOUNTAINS OF
IRELAND

by

Paddy Dillon

CICERONE PRESS
MILNTHORPE, CUMBRIA

© Paddy Dillon 1992
ISBN 1 85284 110 9
First published 1993
Reprinted 1996

British Library Cataloguing-in-Publication Data. A catalogue record for
this book is available from the British Library.

Dedicated to
summit baggers everywhere

Advice to Readers

Readers are advised that whilst every effort is taken by the author
to ensure the accuracy of this guidebook, changes can occur
which may affect the contents. It is advisable to check locally on
transport, accommodation, shops etc but even rights-of-way can
be altered and, more especially overseas, paths can be eradicated
by landslip, forest fires or changes of ownership.

The publisher would welcome notes of any such changes

Front Cover: The Comeragh wilderness, looking to Knockanaffrin
and Slievenamon

CONTENTS

When it all goes wrong - send for the Mountain Rescue!

INTRODUCTION

"In the beginning God created the heavens and the earth." (Gen 1.1)

IN IRISH mythology there is no creation account. In the beginning...was Ireland. True, it had only one plain, three lakes and nine rivers, but other landscape features were added later - usually in bizarre circumstances. Partholan was the first man to set foot on the Auld Sod - and it probably went *squelch*! Some things never change.

Partholan had a son called Slanga, who died and was buried on a northern mountain-top which became Sliabh Slainge on that account. Right from the beginning, there was a reverence for the mountains of Ireland. The western mountain of Cruachán Aigle was deemed to be sacred by the druids who performed mysterious rites on its summit. In the south-west of the country, Sliabh Daidche was also venerated.

I mention these three mountains because they were all thoroughly Christianized. Sliabh Slainge was renamed Slieve Donard after a follower of St Patrick. It was St Patrick who fasted and prayed forty days on Cruachán Aigle, which is now called Croagh Patrick. The sailor-saint Brendan put to sea from the foot of Sliabh Daidche, now known as Brandon Mountain in his honour.

The Paps and Caherconree were named after powerful deities. The name of Slievenamon recalls how the women raced up the mountain for the love of the hoary old warrior Finn. The old man himself got around a lot, as witnessed by the number of Seefin - seat of Finn - placenames. The rugged Caha Mountains may once have been named after the Seven Deadly Sins and to this day pilgrims scale the mountains to expiate those same sins. Alas, many of the old tales are lost, but those which remain show how Irish mythology is intimately woven into the Irish landscape. This guide is not about the mountains and their myths - only about the mountains - but remember that there is more to these mountains than meets the eye!

The purpose of this guide is simply to lead the reader to the top of every mountain in Ireland. It is, therefore, a guide for mountain walkers who like to respond to a challenge. There are over 200 mountains in Ireland, which sounds rather daunting, but a very determined and fit walker could cover them all in a month. Mere mortals, however, would prefer to allocate rather more time for the task and should aim to enjoy the experience.

DEFINING AN IRISH MOUNTAIN

The term "mountain" is used to describe all sorts of humps and bumps across the face of Ireland. Height or appearance seem to have nothing to do with the use of the term. It is simply a legacy of the days when the Ordnance Survey - the map-making wing of the British army - translated Irish placenames as they measured the length and breadth of the country. The resulting "mountains" form no part of my definition.

In Scotland there are the *Munros* - mountains above 3,000 feet. There are the *Corbetts* - from 2,500 to 3,000 feet. There are even the *Donalds* - which are summits above 2,000 feet in southern Scotland. These heights are named after those who drew up various tables of heights. In England and Wales, anything above 2,000 feet is generally deemed to be a mountain. You may see a pattern beginning to emerge. Irish landforms are on the same general scale as those in England and Wales, though the overall wilderness aspect is often more akin to Scotland. Lists of Irish mountains above 2,000, 2,500 and 3,000 feet have been published in the past. I'm settling for the 2,000 feet level - anything above that level is an Irish mountain.

2,000 FEET - FROM WHERE?

There is a problem, so I'll try and keep it simple. Basically, the 2,000 feet is measured vertically from sea level, but the sea rises and falls twice daily, so clarification is required. When the Ordnance Survey first mapped Ireland, all the heights were measured from Low Water in Dublin Bay. All the heights I have quoted *in feet* are measured from that point.

Following the partition of Ireland in the 1920s, the Ordnance Survey retired to their British HQ after setting up the Ordnance Survey of Ireland (in Dublin) and the Ordnance Survey of Northern Ireland (in Belfast). These new survey agencies inherited all the heights measured above Low Water in Dublin Bay, but were left to map out their respective territories in any format they wished. The Ordnance Survey of Northern Ireland obtained data on Mean Sea Level at Belfast Lough and measured all their heights from that point. Later, both surveys pooled their skills and calculated the Mean Sea Level at Malin Head. All the new 1:50,000 maps which have been published through the 1980s and 1990s have heights measured in metres above Mean Sea Level at Malin Head.

Here's the problem. If I try to convert an old height from feet into metres, I end up with a value which is greater than the new metric maps admit. Not only that, but there were some mistakes made in the early surveys which are still coming to light.

Here's how I've tried to deal with the problem. First, I've credited all the mountains with their original heights in feet. Second, where new metric heights have been calculated, I've made a note of them. Third, where new metric heights aren't available, I've had a go at guessing what they will be. Obviously, this will need to be tidied up in subsequent editions of the guide, and none of this affects the overall quality of the mountains of Ireland!

HOW MANY 2,000-FOOT MOUNTAINS ARE THERE?

I was determined, right from the start, that not every hump or bump above 2,000 feet would qualify as a separate mountain summit. I toyed with the idea of mathematical formulae designed to exclude the less significant summits, but finally settled for on-site appraisals. Basically, if a summit didn't look or feel separate from its neighbours then I simply didn't list it. Some walkers may feel that I have been too harsh in "removing" summits from the Comeragh Mountains, or may wonder why I have included others elsewhere. Very keen summit baggers will find that I've mentioned most of the "also-ran" heights in the text.

After much deliberation, both on the mountains as well as afterwards, I arrived at a final total of 212 separate mountain summits. I have a tidy mind, so I was disappointed that it didn't turn out to be a nice, round 200. I looked again, and discovered that there were in fact just 200 summits above 2,000 feet - and a further 12 summits above 3,000 feet. That satisfied me immensely!

PADDY'S WAY

Most books dealing with the mountains of Ireland start from the Wicklow Mountains and move from range to range in a clockwise direction to finish on the Mountains of Mourne. If you step back from a relief map of Ireland, you may agree with my general arrangement of mountainous areas: east, south, south-west, west and north. I was happy to fall in line with the usual clockwise progression and conducted my researches in that direction.

Many years ago I made a winter ascent of Carrauntoohil. It was the first Irish mountain I climbed and I thought that the rest would be easy by comparison. I was wrong - but it was great fun being proven wrong! I followed no particular plan, but would sometimes set myself a target, such as visiting the highest point in every county, or climbing every summit on a particular range. The trouble is, if you don't have an overall plan you never seem to get anywhere!

When I decided that a guidebook offering routes to every 2,000-foot summit in Ireland was a good idea, I went straight back to square one. I decided I'd climb the whole lot - even those I'd climbed many times before. I've included brief details of my tour under the heading "Paddy's Way" at the beginning of each of the five sections. I don't expect readers to follow slavishly in my footsteps, but you might be interested in how I structured my approach to what might seem like a Herculean task.

For a start, I walked over 1,200 miles, but the routes in this guide amount to little more than 600 miles. I had to check a number of routes before settling on the ones in this guide. I used public transport, or hitch-hiked from range to range. You could do it much quicker by car. I made three separate tours of about a month apiece, but some of my time was spent on long-distance walking routes such as the Wicklow Way, Kerry Way and Dingle Way. If you were to restrict yourself to the mountain walks, you'd cover the course in less time than it took me. I'm not advocating record-breaking, though that may appeal to someone eventually, but I am advocating a planned approach as being the best way to tackle the ascent of every mountain in Ireland.

Anyway, for the benefit of readers, I show roughly how I travelled from range to range, including notes about where I stayed and what the weather was like. My tour followed roughly the same plan as the layout of this guide, though there were minor differences. All the photographs in the guide were taken while engaged on the tour. If they show anything, they show that it doesn't always rain in Ireland!

THE PLAN OF THIS GUIDE

THE WALK NUMBER

The walks are numbered from 1 to 70 and each walk covers anything from 1 to 9 separate mountain summits which are immediately listed. The walk number ties in with a sketch map bearing the same number, as well as featuring on one of the five area maps showing the distribution of the walks. The mountains covered on each walk are listed in the way you'll find them on the Ordnance Survey maps. In some cases I've had to obtain names from another source, or even had to make up a name. The heights are quoted in both feet and metres, and if you still can't locate the summits I've given six figure grid references.

CHARACTER

I've tried, in a sentence or two, to sum up the character of the mountains and/or the walks over them. This generally indicates the level of difficulty, or any problems which might be encountered.

DISTANCE

The distance of the walks is given in both miles and kilometres. Some walks are circuits, some are "there-and-back", while others are from "A-to-B". The distance covers everything from the start to the finish, whether you finish back where you started, or finish miles away on the far side of a mountain range. You can drive a car to odd summits, so don't need to walk at all! The longest walk described is twenty-four miles.

MAPS

The sketch maps I have drawn are on a scale of 1:50,000. You can make immediate comparisons between the walks, but you can't hope to use these maps on the mountains. The sketch maps show only the outline of the route, the position of the mountain summits and the nearest roads. There are very few other features shown. If I catch anyone trying to navigate with these maps I'll confiscate their guide! You must use the appropriate Ordnance Survey maps.

I have quoted the number of a 1:50,000 map for each of the walks and I urge walkers to use them. In Northern Ireland, these have been available for some years, but in the Republic of Ireland the series is incomplete. At the time of final revision, well over half of the mountains listed are covered by 1:50,000 mapping. Many mountainous areas are being given priority in the production programme.

The other map number I have quoted refers to the Half Inch to One Mile series. In the absence of a 1:50,000 map, these are probably the best alternatives. Only buy the Half Inch map if there is no 1:50,000 map available, then rush to replace it as soon as a new map is published. The Half Inch series, of course, carries all the heights in feet, so they will remain a useful reference series even when all the new metric maps have been published.

In a few cases I have been able to quote the names of some 1:25,000 maps. These are the best that money can buy and if any are listed for your chosen walk I heartily recommend that you use them. It is hoped that further areas will be covered by 1:25,000 mapping in the future, but the ultimate success of all the new Ordnance Survey products depends on people buying and using them.

For general touring purposes, I'd recommend the 1:250,000 Holiday Maps of Ireland. These were published to agreed specifications by both Ordnance Surveys and contain a wealth of incidental detail. They show the mountainous areas clearly and note all the access roads. They are invaluable when touring between the ranges, or seeking remote villages, glens and mountain passes.

START/FINISH

The start of each walk is usually the point you'll return to later. In a few cases, there are long walks through mountain ranges which finish elsewhere. You'll have to arrange to be collected by someone at the end of these walks, or find some way of getting a lift back to the start if you've parked a car there.

GETTING THERE

Just a brief note explaining where the walks start and finish in relation to the nearest towns or villages. Road classification numbers are given which can be checked on maps. It should be remembered that hardly anyone in Ireland refers to the classification numbers, but they are usually featured on all new signposts.

THE ROUTE

This is the part that matters! All the route descriptions are arranged in the same way. First, I take you from the starting point to a mountain summit. If this is a solitary mountain, then I'll usually suggest that you walk back down the same way. If there are more mountains involved, then I'll take you to each summit in turn. After reaching the final summit, a paragraph explains how to conclude the walk, either by returning to the starting point or by aiming for the nearest road.

Throughout all the route descriptions, I've tried to give you the hard information you'll need to reach each of the mountain summits. You may tire of the number of times I've used the word "boggy", but that's the sort of information you'll be glad to have in advance! If there are clear tracks, I'll mention them. If there's a steep and rocky climb, I'll tell you so. I'll let you know if there's a cairn or trig point on the summit, so that you'll know when you've got there! Read the route descriptions carefully before attempting the walks - in one case they may encourage you onwards, while in another case they may warn you of difficulties ahead.

I've also tried to offer translations, and the original Irish forms, of the mountain names. Some names have become so corrupted that they can hardly even be guessed. One of the things you'll notice is that the names are either highly descriptive, or serve to enshrine some element of local folklore. It's a great pity that the new 1:50,000 maps couldn't have been made bilingual. On the other hand, the new 1:25,000 map of Macgillycuddy's Reeks is mostly true to the original Irish forms and is the only map to name all the peaks along the Reeks ridge!

ALTERNATIVES

I offer only a single route in detail, but end each walk by suggesting alternative approaches. These vary. In one instance I may indicate a different way up a mountain. In another I may suggest an easier breakdown of a long, hard walk. Finally, for tough and enthusiastic mountain walkers, I may offer pointers towards long expeditions which can be formed by joining the walks together.

GENERAL INFORMATION

SAFETY ON THE MOUNTAINS

I dislike preaching on this subject. To start with, you need more common sense than anything else. You need to select walks which you know you can complete in a given time and you need to be able to cope with the changing weather. If you start on a sunny, clear day, can you finish the walk in darkness or mist? If you have to scramble along a rocky ridge, have you a good balance and a head for heights?

Equipment is important - both what you wear and what you carry - but opinions and personal preferences vary. You need footwear which can cope with wet, boggy ground, or steep, rocky slopes, or miles of tarmac bashing. You need clothes which will keep you warm and dry. You should carry a map and compass - and know how to use them. In a nutshell, your pack should carry items which will make your journey easy no matter what happens - a torch in case it gets dark, a whistle to attract attention, a first-aid kit for accidents.

Food is important - and again a matter of personal preference. You need enough food to see you round the course. Mountain walking requires a lot of energy. You need extra food in case you're delayed, or have to spend a night on a mountain. If there's no water on the mountain, then you'll need to carry a drink - especially in hot weather. There are tales of "hungry grass", which go like this. The bodies of unbaptised babies and famine victims were often buried on lonely mountainsides. Anyone stepping on these unmarked graves will be seized by a sudden hunger. Hungry grass or not, most mountain walkers will know the feeling!

If the worst comes to the worst and you have an accident, then how's your first aid? If you're on your own with a broken leg, it could be weeks before anyone comes your way. Did you tell anyone where you were going? If you're in a group, then someone can go for help. If you need to be evacuated from the mountain, then that's a job for the mountain rescue team. Alert them through Garda or RUC channels by getting to a phone and dialling 999. Better still, don't get into those situations.

ACCESS

There is no general right of access to the mountains of Ireland. Rights of way may exist in places, but they aren't recorded on maps. For the most part, landowners and farmers seem to have no objection to walkers heading for the heights. It is therefore incumbent on walkers to be considerate and careful while enjoying their mountain treks. When you meet people who live and work on the mountains, you'll find that they often appreciate a bit of conversation. They may not be able to understand *why* you want to climb their mountain, but they'll be able to offer useful advice. It's worth noting that the Ordnance Survey's name for odd mountains may not correspond in the slightest with local usage! Sadly, I must report that large groups of walkers in the Sperrin Mountains have annoyed some of the farmers. Access to Dart Mountain cannot be guaranteed. If you're in doubt about any of the routes, then ask permission.

FLORA

The Wicklow Mountains and the Mountains of Mourne are almost totally lacking in unusual flora, but the south-west of Ireland features a host of odd species. There are several uncommon arctic/alpine plants which are well and truly stranded on the high mountains. Many can be noted on Carrauntoohil and Brandon. Some extremely rare plants can be found on some heights - maybe only known in two or three locations. Ardent botanists will delight to find them.

The south-west is also notable for its range of Hiberno-Lusitanian flora and perhaps the most commonly occurring plant is St Patrick's Cabbage. There's also the Arbutus, or Strawberry Tree, which occurs around the Mediterranean, but is equally at home around Killarney. The south-west is also a stronghold of the Greater Butterwort, which brings colour to many barren bogs. You could also spot Sundews. In the west, St Dabeoc's Heath is a heather you won't find elsewhere in Ireland - another Hiberno-Lusitanian plant.

Many mountains are bald and rocky, or blanketed in bleak bogs, but even in these forbidding locations there may be unusual lichens or mosses which have found a niche. For the most part, however, the mountains of Ireland feature treeless, grassy or heathery moors, where only nodding Cotton Grass provides a highlight.

FAUNA

The mountains of Ireland feature very few birds and mammals. Ravens can be seen over most heights, but other birds tend to have more limited distributions. A few grouse may start from underfoot in the Wicklow

Mountains, but they are comparatively rare elsewhere. Choughs can be noted in the south-west. Skylarks and meadow pipits occur almost everywhere, and lonely loughs will often serve to attract migrant species. Every so often, merlins or peregrines will make a dramatic entrance in the wild places. Despite the number of placename references to eagles, these are totally absent. The exception was a recent visitor from America which crash-landed in the west of Ireland and was flown home in a jumbo jet!

You can see introduced Sika Deer in the Wicklow Mountains, or you could head for the National Parks of Killarney or Glenveagh to see Red Deer. There are few large mammals in the Irish mountains, though you might notice feral goats on inaccessible sea-cliffs, such as on Achill Island. Foxes and hares somehow manage to share the same mountain habitat. Midges and horseflies can be a nuisance in summer, but the rain keeps them down. When it really pours in the south-west, look out for the Kerry Spotted Slug, which is now a protected species. We can thank St Patrick for the fact that there are no snakes in Ireland - but who do we thank for the general lack of species?

PUBLIC TRANSPORT

Getting to Ireland is relatively quick and easy. The quick way is by air and some services from Britain fly direct to western points such as Kerry County Airport or Knock Airport. Rail travel is simply a matter of buying tickets which cover the ferry journey - you can book from any British station straight through to any Irish station. Car drivers can use any of the ferry services: Holyhead to Dublin, Holyhead to Dun Laoghaire, Fishguard to Rosslare, Pembroke to Rosslare, Swansea to Cork, Stranraer to Larne and Cairnryan to Larne. Foot passengers can usually obtain student or YHA discounts if they can show the appropriate cards.

Very few of the mountain walks start from a bus route, and none at all start from a railway station. However, for general travelling from town to town, occasionally passing mountain ranges, you can rely on the buses. In simple terms, routes in the Republic of Ireland are operated by Bus Eireann, while those in Northern Ireland are operated by Ulsterbus. Yellow school buses often operate in remote areas, but generally don't carry passengers. You can check with Tourist Information Offices near your chosen destination to see if any private operators are running services nearer to the mountains.

TRAVELLING BY CAR

This is the most convenient way of reaching the mountains, but parking can be rather tight in many places. If there is a handy car park, then it will be mentioned in the text. If not, then you can drive to the start of the walk, noting any small spaces where you might be able to squeeze a car. Sometimes, minor roads can be very narrow and farm vehicles may need plenty of room. Park considerately, or ask for permission from a nearby house or farm. You can drive to the summits of a few mountains - as high as 2,610 feet on Mount Leinster. If you see any hitch-hikers, then give them a lift - one of them might be me!

ACCOMMODATION

Let's start with hotels and B&Bs, which are available almost everywhere. Many of these places are "approved" by either Bord Fáilte or the Northern Ireland Tourist Board. If you book accommodation through a Tourist Information Office you'll almost certainly be sent to an "approved" place which will meet certain standards. There are other B&Bs which rely on simple roadside advertising and many of these will provide perfectly acceptable accommodation. If they are close to the mountains, then so much the better.

There are several Youth Hostels administered either by An Oige or the Youth Hostels Association of Northern Ireland. Both organisations have lost a number of hostels in recent years - the older your map, the more hostels it will show! Many of those remaining are well placed for the mountains - especially in Co Wicklow and Co Kerry. Members holding a Youth Hostel card issued in any country can simply turn up and ask for accommodation. It's also possible to book ahead. Even non-members can turn up at any hostel and join on the spot.

There's a booming network of Independent Hostels which offer simple accommodation. Most are situated in the south-west, west and north-west, though there are others across Ireland. Most aren't "approved" by Tourist Information Offices, so you'll need to obtain a list of addresses - usually obtainable at any of the hostels. Several of the Independent Hostels are close to the mountains and provide good bases for walkers operating on tight budgets.

If you prefer to carry a tent, then there are very few organised sites near the mountains. If you want a lowland pitch, most farmers will readily oblige. Technically, you should ask for permission to camp on the mountains, but you probably wouldn't know who to ask. Discreet camping on the heights seems to be acceptable, but you'll need to think about your safety in such remote places and you should leave your pitches spotlessly clean. Camping is expressly forbidden in all State Forests and National Parks.

TOURIST INFORMATION OFFICES

Most towns in Ireland have Tourist Information Offices - just look for the "i" sign. Many are administered by Bord Fáilte or the Northern Ireland Tourist Board, but some are simple information points which may be provided by local tourism committees. Most of these places will be able to assist you with details of accommodation, transport and "things to see". Don't expect them to be able to offer you routes up the mountains, though there may be a few local walking guides on sale which you might find useful.

FINALLY

Summit bagging is a game and games are supposed to be enjoyed. Any "rules" I may have laid down defining mountain summits, or any lists I have drawn up, are purely a matter of opinion. If you're playing this game, you're entitled to make up your own rules and adapt any information I'm offering. You might be kind enough to let me know if I've made any glaring errors, missed an obvious route, or forgotten to include a mountain! I would also be most interested to hear from anyone who has covered all the 2,000-foot mountains in Ireland, whether from this list or from any other list. Write to me c/o Cicerone Press giving brief details.

EAST

36 Mountains - 14 Walks

The mountains in the east of Ireland are the Wicklow Mountains and their nearest neighbours, the Blackstairs Mountains. Both ranges are part of a vast block of granite - the Wicklow Granite. Where this bedrock is exposed it usually forms large slabs or boulders, but a vast upland blanket bog covers most of the high ground. The Wicklow Mountains are broad-shouldered, with rounded summits. The overall impression is of bleakness and desolation. Some of the lower glens are quite beautiful - Glendalough and Powerscourt have long been on the tourist trail. Both areas have been protected to form the core of the proposed Wicklow Mountains National Park. When further acquisitions of land have been made, the national park will stretch from Tonduff to Lugnaquillia along the main axis of the Wicklow Mountains.

Despite rising from the suburbs of Dublin, the Wicklow Mountains provided, for many centuries, a safe haven for wild tribes, warriors, rebels and outlaws. Only after the 1798 Rebellion was authority finally stamped on the area. The British Army laboured through the Wicklow wilderness to build the Military Road through the heart of the mountains. The route is a splendid scenic drive these days and it gives access to many fine, high-level walks.

Although the Wicklow Mountains can be wild and inhospitable, they are also easily accessible to Dubliners and it's not uncommon to find large groups marching through the bleakest of bogs. The Wicklow Way - the first fully waymarked long-distance walking route in Ireland - was taken through the mountains to pass Djouce, Mullacor and Croaghanmoira. Like the Military Road, the Wicklow Way offers easy access to and from the mountains. Linked with the South Leinster Way, it offers a route from the Wicklow Mountains to the Blackstairs Mountains.

PADDY'S WAY - EAST

I started my tour of the Irish mountains by following the Wicklow Way from Dublin. There was still snow in the air and sharp frosts in the morning. Spring was late. My plan was fairly simple - I wanted to follow the Wicklow Way in stages, taking two or three days off from time to time

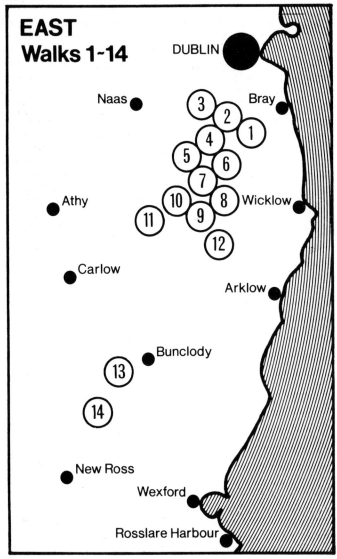

to explore the mountains. Basing myself at Knockree and Glencree Youth Hostels, I covered the northern groups of mountains first, north of the Sally Gap.

After crossing the Sally Gap and walking to Mullaghcleevaun in the company of a walker from Dublin, I made Glendalough Youth Hostel my base for a few days. I walked over some fairly easy mountains from the scenic glen, then followed the Wicklow Way over to Glenmalure. Over the next couple of days, I walked the circuit of the Glen of Imaal and stayed at Ballinclea Youth Hostel. After a long day picking off odd summits here and there, I retired to Aghavannagh Youth Hostel.

The Wicklow Mountains were hard work, involving plenty of bogtrotting and wading through deep heather. I was quite tired, so enjoyed a couple of easier days finishing the Wicklow Way and staying in little B&Bs for a change. I continued along part of the South Leinster Way, then left it to make the full traverse of the Blackstairs Mountains - a route which deserves to become a classic. I ended the walk in darkness, threw my sleeping bag down in a field, then got a lift onwards to reach the mountains of the south.

WALK 1:

Summits:	White Hill	2,075ft (630m)	O 179089
	Djouce Mountain	2,385ft (725m)	O 179103
	War Hill	2,250ft (686m)	O 169113

Character:	Three boggy, heathery mountains dominated by Djouce, where many Dubliners have taken their first steps into the hills. The Wicklow Way has been routed through this group, offering easy access.
Distance:	7½ miles (12 kilometres).
Maps:	1:50,000 Sheet 56. Half Inch Sheet 16.
Start/Finish:	Luggala Wood car park.
Getting There:	Luggala Wood is on the R759 road between Roundwood and Sally Gap, overlooking Lough Tay.

THE ROUTE

White Hill

From the car park, head straight into Luggala Wood. A Wicklow Way sign points along a forest track and waymarks indicate left, left again, then right to reveal a path leading onto moorland. Climb uphill past J.B.Malone's granite memorial, which records him as the "Pioneer of the Wicklow Way". Follow the Wicklow Way along an unplanted moorland crest and cross a stile. Keep going uphill, following a path through tussocky grass and heather, passing the rusting remains of an old fence. The summit of White Hill is fairly unremarkable, being grass and heather punctuated by a small rock.

Djouce Mountain (dubh ais = black back)

Keep to the Wicklow Way, which descends from White Hill to reach a boggy gap. It continues down to Powerscourt Waterfall, so we must abandon it on the gap. Our route continues uphill on firm ground, still following the line of old fenceposts. As the path levels out it reaches a prominent straining post. Turn right at this point and walk to the top of Djouce. The summit trig point is perched on one of a series of rocky fangs. Views take in the desolate Wicklow Mountains, but also look over gentle coastal country.

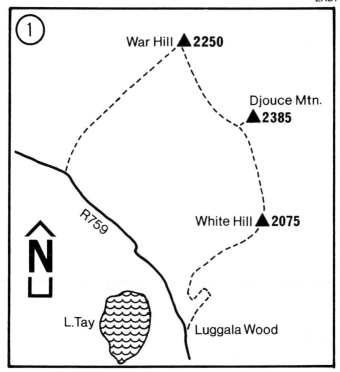

War Hill (an bharr = the top)

Walk back to the straining post on the shoulder of Djouce, then continue to trace the line of old fenceposts downhill. A boggy path leads through the heather, passing an area of large granite blocks. The peculiar shape of one of these has earned it the name of Coffin Stone. Cross a wide, boggy gap, then trace the path and fenceposts up the slopes of the pudding-like War Hill. The summit has only a small cairn.

You can either retrace your steps to return to Luggala Wood, or walk downhill on a south-westwards course to reach the R759 road. If this latter option is chosen, note that there is no path across the heathery wastes. When the road is reached, turn left and walk uphill to return to Luggala Wood, enjoying fine views across Lough Tay to the rugged face of Fancy Mountain.

Alternatives:
A splendid scenic start can include the Powerscourt Waterfall, using the Wicklow Way to reach White Hill and Djouce. It's also possible to continue from War Hill to Tonduff, or even Kippure, but you'll need to be picked up by someone at the end of the day. There are no aids to navigation between War Hill and Tonduff - just a huge, featureless bog.

WALK 2:

Summits:	Tonduff	2,107ft (642m)	O 159137
	Kippure	2,475ft (757m)	O 116154
Character:	Two bleak and boggy mountains with very different access routes. Tonduff is reached after a boggy thrash, while Kippure is reached by a simple road-walk to a TV mast.		
Distance:	8 miles (13 kilometres).		
Maps:	1:50,000 Sheet 56. Half Inch Sheet 16.		
Start/Finish:	Near Liffey Head Bridge.		
Getting There:	Liffey Head Bridge is on the R115 road between Glencree and Sally Gap, but isn't very prominent.		

THE ROUTE

Tonduff (tóin dubh = black back)
A short bog-road leads south-eastwards from the R115 road near Liffey Head Bridge. It quickly expires in turf cuttings, leaving walkers to navigate through some awkward bog. Aim for the broad grass and heather slopes of Tonduff, turning eastwards, then north-eastwards on featureless ground to follow the moorland crest. The summit area is a mess of peat hags - some bearing small cairns. Scout around and choose the one you consider to be the highest, then retrace your steps to the R115 road.

Kippure (ciop mhór = big grassy place)
Not far northwards from the bog-road on Tonduff is the access road for the TV mast on Kippure. The narrow road starts from the R115 road at a point where bushes flank a locked gate. Vehicles are prohibited, but

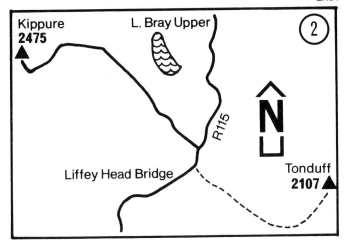

walkers can follow this simple zig-zag route. Even in deep snow, marker posts flanking the road show the way to the top. The tall TV mast marks journey's end, though there is a trig point nearby, in the fenced enclosure. The broad summit is covered in loose grit worn from the granite, and much black peat. Kippure has the distinction of being the highest point in Co Dublin. Walk back down the access road to return to the R115 road.

Alternatives:
You can make life hard for yourself by approaching Tonduff and Kippure from any other directions. Tonduff can be linked with War Hill and Walk 1 by crossing a wide, featureless, boggy gap. Kippure can be linked to Seefingan and Walk 3 by crossing a very broad and boggy gap, following a boundary ditch which can only be traced confidently in clear weather.

WALK 3:

Summits:	Seahan	2,131ft (648m)	O 081197
	Corrig Mountain	2,035ft (618m)	O 091194
	Seefingan	2,364ft (724m)	O 087170
	Seefin	2,043ft (621m)	O 074163

Character:	Four rounded, boggy mountains, three of which are crowned with burial cairns. A fine circuit, but note that the walk is around the fringe of Kilbride Military Camp. Check whether firing is taking place on (01) 582169.
Distance:	7 miles (11 kilometres).
Maps:	1:50,000 Sheet 56. Half Inch Sheet 16.
Start/Finish:	At the entrance to Kilbride Military Camp.
Getting There:	The Camp can be approached from Kippure House or Kilbride - both on the R579 road - or from Dublin via the R114 road. Minor roads lead to the entrance.

THE ROUTE

Seahan (suí Chon = seat of Conn)

Check the state of the firing range before attempting this walk - if in doubt then leave the circuit for another day. Follow a minor road northwards from the entrance of Kilbride Military Camp. Cross a small stream on the right-hand side of the road to reach the edge of a forest. A bulldozed track accompanies the forest fence away from the road, leading to a high corner of the forest. When the track turns left at the corner, simply continue uphill across open moorland. A short walk across grass and heather quickly leads to the top of Seahan. A trig point has been mounted on the large, blocky summit cairn. Views embrace both the Wicklow Mountains and the city of Dublin.

Corrig Mountain (carraig = rock)

Don't follow a trodden path away from Seahan, but aim straight for Corrig Mountain. The boundary of the Kilbride Military Camp is marked by granite blocks inscribed WD (War Department) and these are useful navigational aids in mist. It should be admitted that the markers are out of date as the War Department changed its name to the Department of Defence. The route crosses wet ground, both on the gap as well as on top of Corrig Mountain. A WD block and a couple of metal posts mark the summit.

Seefingan (suí Fingan = seat of Fingan)

The way southwards from Corrig Mountain is a gradual, gentle descent

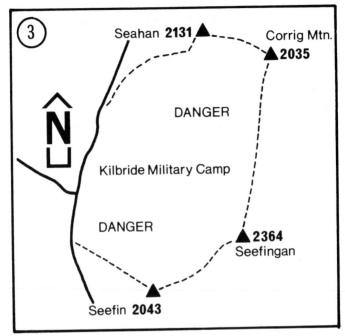

on wet ground. A wide, boggy gap has to be crossed. Beyond the gap, roughly parallel to a line of WD blocks, is a fairly well trodden path. This leads uphill to a broad, boggy area. Slightly off the summit of Seefingan, yet managing to rise higher than it, is a colossal, bouldery burial cairn surmounted by a WD block. The Prehistoric builders obviously chose their site so that it would be visible from below, as any structure on the true summit would have been hidden from sight.

Seefin (suí Finn = seat of Finn)
A vague path leads south-westwards from Seefingan, crossing areas of heather and grass on the descent. Drainage ditches and a forest fence cross a boggy gap. A short, easy ascent leads to the summit of Seefin. Another huge cairn has been constructed just off the summit - this time with a passage leading to a central chamber. From the top of the cairn there is a good view over Dublin's river - the Liffey.

Follow the range boundary roughly north-westwards to descend. This course isn't obvious over the steep, rugged, heathery slopes, but a forest fence later offers a sure guide to the road below. Turn right to follow the road back to the entrance of Kilbride Military Camp.

Alternatives:
These four summits offer such a neat circuit that it seems pointless to suggest alternative ascents. However, there is scope for extending the walk from Seefingan to Kippure. This route crosses a very broad and boggy gap, following a boundary ditch which can only be traced confidently in clear weather.

WALK 4:

Summits:	Carrigvore	2,244ft (682m)	O 123101
	Gravale	2,352ft (718m)	O 105094
	Duff Hill	2,364ft (720m)	O 094083
	Mullaghcleevaun		
	East Top	2,615ft (790m)	O 082067
	Mullaghcleevaun	2,788ft (847m)	O 068071

Character:	A trek over five mountain summits to the heart of the Wicklow Mountains. Each vast, heathery hump is followed by a higher one. It's a rough and boggy succession, ending with a long walk along the Military Road.
Distance:	15 miles (24 kilometres).
Maps:	1:50,000 Sheet 56. Half Inch Sheet 16.
Start/Finish:	Sally Gap.
Getting There:	Sally Gap is a remote crossroads reached via the R115 road from Glencree, the R759 road from Kilbride or Roundwood, or the Military Road from Laragh.

THE ROUTE

Carrigvore (carraig mhór = big rock)
From the crossroads at Sally Gap, take a run at the steep slope to the south-west. There is deep heather, which is immediately dispiriting, but

Rocky outcrops on the summit of Djouce (Walk 1)
Granite boulders near the summit of Gravale (Walk 4)

Wicklow mountain scenery from Clohernagh (Walk 9)
The flat-topped, steep-sided Comeragh Mountains (Walk 16)

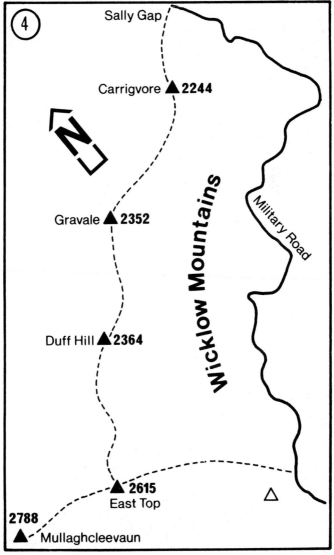

a good path appears quite suddenly. This leads up to an old boundary ditch, which can be followed to provide the firmest footing. The stony ditch leads to a rather blank summit where only a few boulders lie scattered around.

Gravale (gairbhéal = gravel)

The boundary ditch can be traced down from Carrigvore, but runs into boggy patches in the heather. After crossing a gap, an ascent leads to a level, boggy area, then there is another short uphill stretch. The summit is marked with a cairn and there are some large boulders nearby. Views in all directions are bleak and desolate.

Duff Hill (dubh = black)

The descent from Gravale passes between some large boulders, then continues down a rough slope to reach a boggy gap. An uphill slog takes in a steep, rough, almost corrugated slope and we'll probably all agree that this is the toughest part of the day's walk. The slope gradually levels out, the corrugations smooth out, and the summit has a cairn and a scattering of boulders. Catch your breath while taking in the sweeping views.

Mullaghcleevaun East Top

The walk down from Duff Hill is fairly easy, then after crossing a broad gap a gentle ascent begins. The peaty surface has worn away in places, so that a firm footing can be found on grass or stones. The broad moorland crest snakes gradually uphill and a minor rise is crossed on the way to the summit. There is a cairn amid some large blocks of granite.

Mullaghcleevaun (mullach chliabháin = summit of the cradle)

A short descent from the East Top leads to a broad gap almost denuded of vegetation. Take a line avoiding the softer patches, then climb the broad crest leading onto the shoulders of Mullaghcleevaun. The broad top of the mountain is covered in short grass - a pleasant change from thrashing about in bogs and heather. There is a trig point marking the summit, a few granite blocks and a small memorial. Good views take in the huge, heathery rises which constitute the Wicklow Mountains - a scene of utter desolation, with us standing at the heart of it.

Backtrack to Mullaghcleevaun East Top, then take a line roughly south-eastwards for a long descent. A forest edge leads down to the Military Road. Turn left to follow this narrow, twisting line through the forest and out across the moors. Despite its seemingly endless gyrations, it eventually returns to Sally Gap. It's useful if you can arrange to be collected as soon as you reach the road, or you could hitch-hike back to Sally Gap.

Alternatives:
If the wilderness appeals to you, then consider connecting this walk with some other walks in the vicinity. Northwards, a rugged link could be forged with Kippure's summit. Westwards lie Moanbane and Silsean - detailed in Walk 5. By heading southwards it's possible to reach Tonelagee and Walk 6. This last option could be quite difficult as there is a long ridge of peat hags to negotiate. The usual way to avoid it is to walk just to the east side of the ridge, where the slope begins to steepen, taking advantage of an easier grassy strip known as the Green Road.

WALK 5:

Summits:	Silsean	2,296ft (698m)	O 023056
	Moanbane	2,313ft (703m)	O 034069
Character:	Two rather featureless moorland humps above Glenbride. The walk over them is fairly easy.		
Distance:	6 miles (10 kilometres).		
Maps:	1:50,000 Sheet 56. Half Inch Sheet 16.		
Start/Finish:	On the Glenbride Lodge access road.		
Getting There:	Glenbride is half way between Blessington Reservoir and the Wicklow Gap, off the R756 road.		

THE ROUTE

Silsean (soilseán = place of lights)
Follow the access road towards Glenbride Lodge (formerly a youth hostel and shooting lodge), but if driving a car, then park before entering a forest. Walk into the forest, then take a track on the left which may have a barrier across it. Take the next rough track on left and follow this uphill through the forest, crossing straight over another track. Exit onto open moorland at the first opportunity and keep right along the forest edge. A fence leads straight up the heathery slope. This is a useful guide at first, but you must later cross an expanse of grassland to reach the top of

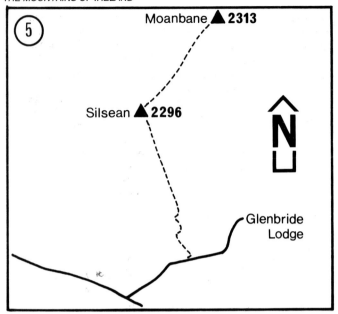

Silsean. The summit is a squelchy area of grass with no distinguishing marks. There is a good view of the Wicklow Gap.

Moanbane (móin bhán = white bog)
The broad moorland crest heading roughly north-eastwards from Silsean to Moanbane is quite wet. There are small pools across the wide gap between the two summits. Even the summit of Moanbane could be said to bear a pool, in the absence of any other features. Blessington Reservoir can be seen to the west, while Mullaghcleevaun is the broad rise to the east. Retrace steps to Glenbride.

Alternatives:
The route can be continued eastwards from Moanbane to reach Mullaghcleevaun. There is a long, broad, wet moorland crest which effects the link. Firmer footing is available on the slopes of Mullaghcleevaun, then a number of routes could be considered from that central hub, as listed at the end of Walk 4.

WALK 6:

Summits:	Tonelagee	2,686ft (817m)	O 085016
	Scarr	2,108ft (641m)	O 133018
Character:	Two rugged mountains which can be tackled together from the Glenmacnass Waterfall. Both ascents have difficult starts, but the higher parts offer easier walking.		
Distance:	8¹/₂ miles (14 kilometres).		
Maps:	1:50,000 Sheet 56. Half Inch Sheet 16.		
Start/Finish:	Glenmacnass Waterfall car park.		
Getting There:	Glenmacnass Waterfall lies beside the Military Road between Laragh and Sally Gap. The car park is on top.		

THE ROUTE

Tonelagee (tóin le gaoth = back to the wind)

Tonelagee is flanked by two minor summits which I haven't listed as separate mountains - they are too small and crouch humbly at the feet of Tonelagee. However, I'm offering a route which includes them - a fine circuit above Lough Ouler. The walk starts from the car park above Glenmacnass Waterfall. Walk a short way up the river to find useful stepping stones, then cross. Head straight up a steep, heathery slope. This is followed by an easier slope which becomes rather more boggy as height is gained. One of the satellite summits is crossed and the slight descent to a bare, stony gap allows a view of the heart-shaped Lough Ouler. A steep, punishing slope follows, which is littered with boulders. After pauses for breath, the slope begins to level out and we finally reach the stony top of Tonelagee. There is a summit trig point and a cairn. Descend via a much gentler slope running northwards to find a safe descent to Lough Ouler from a bare, stony gap. (The other satellite summit could be reached easily from the gap beforehand.) After reaching the outflow of Lough Ouler, contour around the slopes to rejoin the line which we used for the ascent. Simply walk back down to the car park above Glenmacnass Waterfall.

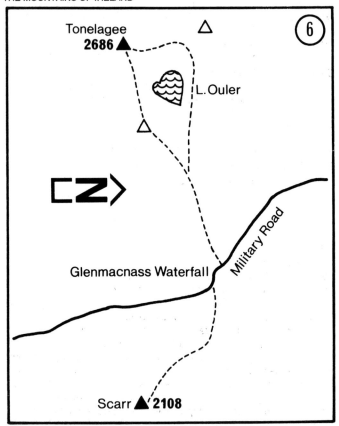

Scarr (sceir = sharp peak)

Walk a short way down the road from the top of the Glenmacnass Waterfall - no further than the second roadside shelter. Look uphill to locate a perched boulder on the skyline and climb the steep, rugged slope to reach it. Bracken is replaced by heather on the ascent and some areas are quite wet. There is a steep slope to tackle just before reaching the perched boulder. Beyond the boulder, easier, gentler moorland slopes are found, and a path eventually encountered. Cross a fence, then climb a steeper slope to reach a narrow ridge bearing a trodden path. There is nothing to mark the summit of Scarr, apart from knobbly parts of the ridge. Turn around and walk back down to the Glenmacnass Waterfall.

Alternatives:

Scarr is rather out on a limb and can't really be linked with any mountain other than Tonelagee. If climbing Scarr simply for its own sake, then there is a good route available from Lough Dan. Tonelagee has an easier side - the rather dull slope rising from the Wicklow Gap. Thus, links are easily forged between Tonelagee and Turlough Hill. A more difficult line links Tonelagee to Mullaghcleevaun. The long moorland crest between the two mountains is covered in peat hags. The usual way of avoiding this is to walk just to the east side of the ridge, where the slope begins to steepen, taking advantage of an easier grassy strip known as the Green Road.

WALK 7:

Summits:	Turlough Hill	2,228ft (681m)	T 063983
	Camaderry	2,296ft (698m)	T 082981
Character:	Easy road access to two mountain summits which are otherwise quite difficult to visit. Unfortunately, the whole area is spoilt by the "Pumped Storage Scheme".		
Distance:	7 miles (11 kilometres).		
Maps:	1:50,000 Sheet 56. Half Inch Sheet 16.		
Start/Finish:	Wicklow Gap.		
Getting There:	The Wicklow Gap is on the highest part of the R756 road between Laragh and Hollywood.		

THE ROUTE

Turlough Hill (turlach = seasonal lake)
The ascent of this mountain is easy and can be completed in most weather conditions, though the road could be lost beneath deep snow. From the top of the Wicklow Gap, a narrow tarmac road heads southwards. This is part of the hydro-electric Pumped Storage Scheme and vehicles are prohibited. You could join a guided tour run by the ESB

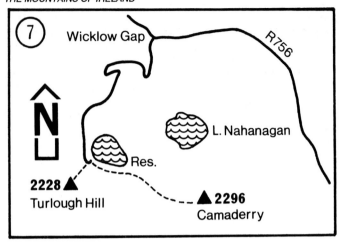

and get a free lift to this summit in a minibus! The road climbs uphill in a series of zig-zags and reaches a reservoir which is overlooked by a concrete tower. This is undoubtedly the highest point on the mountain, but in no way can it be said to be a mountain summit! The reservoir is enclosed by a tall fence, so there's no further access. By way of consolation, I've picked out a minor summit just to the south-west of the reservoir. The ground is disturbed and has been quarried, while a small building and a mast have been placed nearby. However, if you turn your back on the world of schemes and gadgets you could convince yourself that you're on a real mountain. The westward view is bleak enough.

Camaderry (ceim an doire = pass of the oakwood)
Head back to the reservoir and keep to the right-hand side of it. Follow the enclosure fence at first, then cross a broad and rugged gap. There is a vague path threading a way through peaty channels and bouldery patches. The ascent of Camaderry is easier, being a fairly short and gentle climb. The top of the mountain is broad, heathery and bouldery. A large block of granite could be said to mark the summit. There is a nearby rise which some might claim was a separate summit, but it's really only a shoulder of Camaderry. Walk back to the reservoir - which looks like the cone of a volcano - and follow the access road down to the Wicklow Gap.

Alternatives:
Camaderry can be climbed from Glendalough, allowing some splendid scenery to be included in the walk. The ascent in this case would, however, be long, steep and rugged. It's also possible to walk from Turlough Hill to Conavalla, crossing one of the most desolate parts of the Wicklow Mountains. In mist, the only real aid to navigation is the tiny Lough Firrib, where a significant change of direction is required. A challenging circuit could be arranged from Glendalough, crossing Camaderry, Turlough Hill, Conavalla, Lugduff and Mullacor, returning to Glendalough through the forests.

WALK 8:

Summits:	Mullacor	2,179ft (657m)	T	093939
	Lugduff	2,154ft (652m)	T	072954
	Conavalla	2,421ft (734m)	T	040972
Character:	A steep, forested climb along the Wicklow Way, followed by three increasingly difficult mountain summits on a broad, rugged, boggy moorland crest.			
Distance:	13 miles (21 kilometres).			
Maps:	1:50,000 Sheet 56. Half Inch Sheet 16.			
Start/Finish:	Ballinafunshoge, in Glenmalure.			
Getting There:	Glenmalure is served by a minor road which can be reached from Laragh, Rathdrum or Aghavannagh.			

THE ROUTE

Mullacor (mullach mór = big summit)
Follow the road into Glenmalure from the pub at Drumgoff Bridge. When forestry plantations rise on both sides of the road, there is a car park on the right-hand side of the road. A steeply zig-zagging series of tracks have been linked on the forested slopes to provide a route for the Wicklow Way. Look out for markers as you climb and follow these uphill and out of the forest onto the shoulder of Mullacor. The Wicklow Way turns right and heads across Mullacor. The summit is an area of wet grass with a solitary post and is the highest point gained along the course of the Wicklow Way.

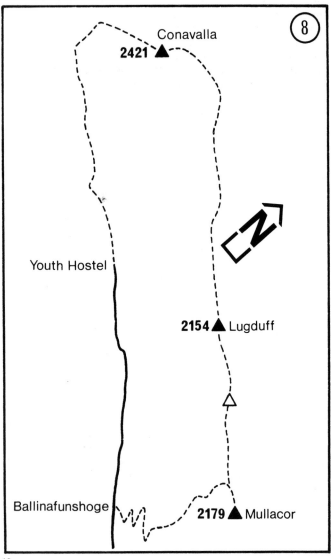

Lugduff (log dubh = black hollow)
Backtrack along the Wicklow Way, down the shoulder of Mullacor, then cross a gap between forestry plantations rising from Glenmalure and Glendalough. The gap is a little boggy, but the ascent beyond is generally firm. A path leads up through a ruined fence and heads straight uphill on grass and heather. There is a broad rise crossed before Lugduff, but it doesn't really count as a separate summit. The true summit is marked with a cairn.

Conavalla (ceann an bhealach = head of the road)
The descent north-westwards along the broad crest of Lugduff runs into bogs and boulders. A broad rise is crossed - hardly a separate summit - then a rugged descent leads to a boggy gap. Any vague paths which may have been traced so far will be lost. You'll have to look ahead carefully to gauge the best line as we're in rather rough country. Pass a cairn while tackling the next ascent, then swing gradually westwards for Conavalla, crossing a series of awkward peaty channels. The broad top of Conavalla is liberally sprinkled with boulders and features isolated peat hags. Some of the hags seem to stand higher than the summit cairn.

The best descent is westwards, down a rugged slope until a small stream is reached. Cross the stream, then walk southwards to join a prominent track. This is the Table Track, which runs over from the Glen of Imaal to Glenmalure. It improves on the descent, becoming a forest road passing the remote Glenmalure Youth Hostel. Continue through the glen to return to the starting point. This part of the route can, of course, be adapted by walkers staying at the Youth Hostel.

Alternatives:
Mullacor can be climbed via the Wicklow Way from Glendalough. A neat little circuit can be enjoyed by adding Lugduff to this approach, returning to Glendalough via Lugduff Spink. Adding Conavalla to the circuit makes for a much more difficult walk, though it's quite possible for tough walkers to continue onwards to make a complete circuit of either Glendalough or Glenmalure.

WALK 9:

Summits:	Clohernagh	2,623ft (800m)	T 058919
	Corrigasleggaun	2,534ft (794m)	T 048911
Character:	Two mountain summits lying on broad spurs from lofty Lugnaquillia, offering a short, high-level circuit.		
Distance:	7½ miles (12 kilometres).		
Maps:	1:50,000 Sheet 56. Half Inch Sheet 16.		
Start/Finish:	Ballinafunshoge, in Glenmalure.		
Getting There:	Glenmalure is served by a minor road which can be reached from Laragh, Rathdrum or Aghavannagh.		

THE ROUTE

Clohernagh (clochernach = stony place)

If starting from the same car park as Walk 8, then walk back down Glenmalure a short way by road, turning right to follow a track across a bridge over the river. Beyond a cottage is an obvious zig-zag track slashed across the mountainside. Some parts of the track are rather wet, but the way uphill is always clear. Eventually, the track ends, leaving us on a steep and rugged slope. There is still a path of sorts, which keeps to the rocky edge overlooking Glenmalure. Continue uphill to reach a prominent cairn. This isn't the summit - it merely stands at a point where a heathery slope changes into a stony plateau. The true summit is

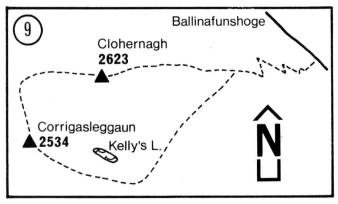

somewhere on the plateau. I've looked long and hard at Clohernagh and will admit that there isn't a great gap between it and Lugnaquillia, but it does stand some distance from the larger mountain and i think it achieves some measure of separateness on that account.

Corrigasleggaun

A short, gentle descent on firm ground leads to a shallow gap, followed by the beginnings of a climb towards Lugnaquillia. We're not going to that mighty summit on this walk, so drift to the left of the broad crest, descending from a cairn. After crossing a lower gap, an ascent leads across some peaty ground to reach the summit cairn on Corrigasleggaun. Note how well crystallised the granite is in this area - allowing individual minerals to be seen.

The descent can be made by following the steep edge overlooking Kelly's Lough. Eventually, it's possible to walk down steep, rugged slopes and cross Carrawaystick Brook. Unfortunately, newly-planted trees may eventually close this line. By contouring around the slopes of Clohernagh, the path used for the ascent will be encountered. Simply follow the path and zig-zag back into Glenmalure via the prominent mountainside track.

Alternatives:

Obviously, either of the two summits could be crossed on the way to or from Lugnaquillia. It's also possible for walkers to use a series of forest tracks rising from near Drumgoff Bridge, which lead most of the way to Kelly's Lough.

WALK 10:

Summits:	Ballineddan Mountain	2,151ft (652m)	T 003908
	Slievemaan	2,501ft (759m)	T 018908
	Lugnaquillia	3,039ft (925m)	T 032918
	Camenabologue East Top	2,175ft (663m)	T 037954
	Camenabologue	2,495ft (758m)	T 023960
	Table Mountain	2,302ft (700m)	T 020973
	Lobawn	2,097ft (636m)	T 979978

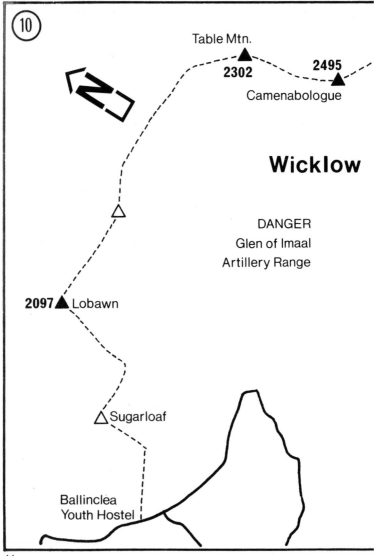

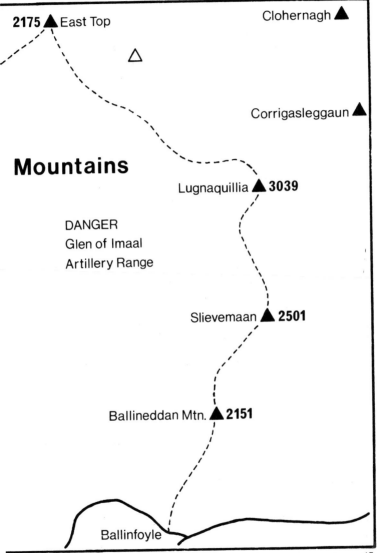

Clohernagh ▲

2175 ▲ East Top

△

Corrigasleggaun ▲

Mountains

Lugnaquillia ▲ 3039

DANGER
Glen of Imaal
Artillery Range

Slievemaan ▲ 2501

Ballineddan Mtn. ▲ 2151

Ballinfoyle

Character:	A long and hard walk over seven mountain summits. This is basically the classic circuit of the Glen of Imaal. Once you start the walk you are largely committed to it. Descents into the Glen of Imaal cannot be made when there is firing on the Artillery Range. Phone for information on (01) 509854, or check locally for displayed schedules.
Distance:	13¹⁄₂ miles (22 kilometres).
Maps:	1:50,000 Sheet 56. Half Inch Sheet 16.
Start:	Ballinfoyle.
Finish:	Ballinclea.
Getting There:	Ballinfoyle and Ballinclea are in the Glen of Imaal, which can be approached from Donard, Baltinglass, Rathdangan or Aghavannagh via minor roads.

THE ROUTE

Ballineddan Mountain (baile an fheadáin = homestead of the stream)
Starting from the lonely road junction at Ballinfoyle, note the sign warning of firing around the Glen of Imaal. The walk described always keeps just to the edge of the range boundary. The walk starts where a gate gives access to an unplanted strip between two newly-planted forests on the lower slopes of Ballineddan Mountain. A short track and fence run uphill, then a path leads up to a band of heather. Simply walk straight uphill, eventually joining a path which leads straight to the summit cairn.

Slievemaan (sliabh meáin = middle mountain)
Although the summit of Slievemaan lies directly eastwards of Ballineddan Mountain, it's better to walk more north-east to cross a gap. This is all on firm ground, rising past a band of boulders and continuing along a gradually rising crest to reach a peaty summit bearing a cairn.

Lugnaquillia (log na coille = hollow of the cocks)
Descend north-eastwards from Slievemaan to cross a level gap of black peat. The ascent is grassy, with several broken rock outcrops. It may be steep, but it's also fairly easy and all you need to do is aim for a prominent block of rock on the skyline. From there, a trodden path rises up a gentle slope of short grass, levelling out on a broad summit. A huge platform

has been built from stones, with a trig point, view indicator and sign warning about the firing range completing the summit furniture. The indicator helps to sort out the extensive panorama, which reaches far beyond the Wicklow Mountains in optimum conditions. Lugnaquillia is the highest point in Co Wicklow, as well as in the Province of Leinster. Out of sight, but important to note, are the North and South Prisons - two cliffs which appear very suddenly if you scout around the edges of the summit plateau.

Camenabologue East Top

Take care on the descent from Lugnaquillia in mist. There is a path leading gently downhill in a north-eastwards direction. This swings more north-westwards later, then you should walk northwards across the minor hump of Cannow. I don't class Cannow as a separate summit and there are other odd humps and bumps nearby which only the most ardent summit-bagger would want to tick off. The only summit off the main ridge which really calls for attention is a rugged, heathery rise overlooking Glenmalure. It has no paths leading to it, and no name either, but after crossing a few boggy patches to reach it, the summit bears a small cairn.

Camenabologue (ceim na mbulog = pass of the bullock)

Walk westwards from the East Top and descend rugged, heathery slopes to reach a broad, boggy gap. Climb up the heathery slope beyond the gap, later crossing areas of grass and stones. There is no path, but gentle slopes finally lead to a large summit cairn.

Table Mountain

A sparse line of waymark posts lead northwards from Camenabologue. There are isolated peat hags on the descent, but most of the peat has gone, leaving a surface of grass and stones. The Table Track, running from Glenmalure to the Glen of Imaal, is crossed near a large warning sign. Note that short-cuts down into the Glen of Imaal are only possible when there is no firing on the Artillery Range. Cross straight over the Table Track, then pick a way across near-level expanses of black peat to reach a small cairn on the broad summit of Table Mountain.

Lobawn (log bhán = white hollow)

A boundary ditch can be traced roughly northwards from the summit of Table Mountain. This gradually turns westwards as it descends in stages to two low gaps. There is plenty of wet and boggy ground on this long walk, then the boundary ditch climbs all the way up the side of Lobawn in one straight line. There are areas of heather and wet grass on top. The summit of Lobawn is marked by a block of granite inscribed WD (meaning War Department).

A descent can be made roughly southwards from the summit. A long, broad ridge is followed, then a sudden turn to the right leads along a broad, heathery crest. This reaches a cairn on the heathery rise called Sugarloaf. Walk southwards again, following a steep path down to an old fence. The rest of the descent involves crossing fences, so look ahead carefully to locate stiles and gates. Aim either for the road junction at Ballinclea, or for the youth hostel. If you have transport or accommodation at this point, then the walk is over. If you have to return to the road junction at Ballinfoyle, perhaps to pick up a car, then you've a lengthy tarmac bash still to do.

Alternatives:
A shorter circuit can be accomplished by using the Table Track to descend into the Glen of Imaal, but there must be no firing on the Artillery Range. Some of the summits can be gained from Glenmalure, and in this case the Table Track can be used in safety. Lobawn is out on a limb and could be visited separately from the other summits. Lugnaquillia, being of noble height, is often climbed simply for its own sake and can be approached from either the Glen of Imaal, Glenmalure, or even Aghavannagh. The shortest and simplest route is via Camarahill - an easy crest which rises from within the Artillery Range, thus limiting its use. Strong walkers could cheerfully set off on the route I have described, but opt to finish somewhere far distant, such as Glendalough or the Wicklow Gap, but mere mortals would shudder at the thought of such extended bogtrots.

WALK 11:

Summit:	Keadeen Mountain 2,146ft (652m) S 953898
Character:	A short, steep climb to a solitary summit.
Distance:	4 miles (6 kilometres).
Maps:	1:50,000 Sheets 56 & 62. Half Inch Sheet 16.
Start/Finish:	Dwyer's Cottage.

Getting There: Dwyer's Cottage is signposted throughout the Glen of Imaal and can be reached via Donard or Aghavannagh.

THE ROUTE

Keadeen Mountain (céidín = flat-topped hill)

There is a car park at Dwyer's Cottage - once home of a notable patriot, or rebel, depending on your point of view. A visit to the cottage can be combined with an ascent of Keadeen Mountain. Walk back down the road, in the direction of Donard, until a stream has been crossed. Turn left to follow a track into a forest. Abandon this track as soon as it swings to the right. Walk straight uphill, walking between the closely packed trees. Eventually, it's better to cross the forest fence and walk uphill alongside it. Bracken-clad slopes come to an end when a wall is crossed at the top end of the forest. The grassy slopes on the upper part of the mountain gradually ease, finally giving way to a level top. The summit is crossed by a fence and bears a trig point and a sprawling cairn. Views all around are very good, as Keadeen mountain stands between the Wicklow Mountains and the broad plains. Reverse the ascent route to return to Dwyer's Cottage.

Alternatives:

You could also walk eastwards from the summit to return to Dwyer's Cottage after reaching a minor road. It's also possible to head straight into Walk 10, which is already a long, hard day's walk.

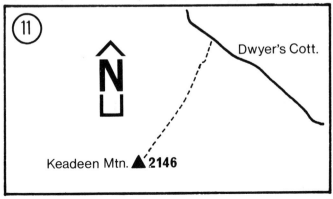

WALK 12:

Summit:	Croaghanmoira 2,181ft (663m) T 098864
Character:	An easy ascent of a solitary summit offering fine views.
Distance:	3 miles (5 kilometres).
Maps:	1:50,000 Sheet 62. Half Inch Sheet 16.
Start/Finish:	On the Military Road.
Getting There:	The Military Road in this area can be approached from Laragh, Glenmalure or Aghavannagh.

THE ROUTE

Croaghanmoira (cruachán maoir = steep-sided mountain of the steward)
Start on the highest part of the Military Road between Glenmalure and
Aghavannagh, which is still free of forestry plantations. There is a gate
on the eastern side of the road near a sheepfold. Follow the nearby
forest fence uphill. This runs up a heathery slope, but there is a bulldozed
track alongside the forest fence which could be used. The plantations
rise almost to the top of Croaghanmoira. The broad slopes of the
mountain end suddenly with a neat, narrow ridge which is crowned with
the summit trig point. The Ordnance Survey took some long sightings
from this place, and provided that the forests don't engulf the summit
there should always be good views available. Follow the forest fence
back down to the Military Road.

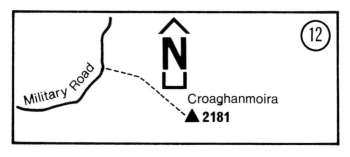

Alternatives:

Despite the intervening forestry plantations, Croaghanmoira could be linked with Lugnaquillia and the surrounding mountains. The Wicklow Way also crosses the shoulders of Croaghanmoira, offering a waymarked route back to some mountains covered earlier in this guide. There's no reason why you shouldn't follow the Wicklow Way in the other direction - towards the Blackstairs Mountains.

WALK 13:

Summit:	Mount Leinster 2,610ft (794m) S 827526
Character:	A mountain which can be as hard or easy to climb as you wish.
Distance:	1¾ miles (3 kilometres).
Maps:	1:50,000 Sheet 68. Half Inch Sheet 19.
Start/Finish:	The Nine Stones.
Getting There:	The Nine Stones can be reached by following minor roads from Bunclody or Borris.

THE ROUTE

Mount Leinster

Do you even need to walk? Most of the time it's possible to drive all the way to the summit using a road which serves a TV mast. This is, however, a private road and vehicular access could be restricted at any time if the gates are locked. There is a parking space beside the Prehistoric Nine Stones, then a simple walk up the access road leads to the summit. There is a tall TV mast, dwarfing a trig point and cairn. Despite its name, this is not the highest point in the Province of Leinster (that honour belongs to Lugnaquillia), but it is the highest point in both Co Carlow and Co Wexford. It's also the highest point you can gain in Ireland without undue difficulty.

Alternatives:

You can measure the true height of the mountain by starting from Kildavin. Follow the waymarked South Leinster Way up the lower slopes, then find a rough, pathless way up to the summit. Another ascent

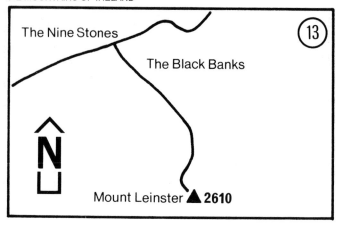

can be made from the Scullogue Gap using a track to the east of Knockroe, then climbing the rough, pathless slopes of the mountain.

WALK 14:

Summit:	Blackstairs Mountain 2,409ft (732m) S 811448
Character:	A rugged ascent of a mountain covered in boulders.
Distance:	6 miles (10 kilometres).
Maps:	1:50,000 Sheet 68. Half Inch Sheet 19.
Start/Finish:	Scullogue Gap.
Getting There:	Scullogue Gap is the highest part of the R702 road between Enniscorthy and Graiguenamanagh.

THE ROUTE

Blackstairs Mountain

Farms and forest seem to block a direct ascent of Blackstairs Mountain from Scullogue Gap. Follow a track into the forest until it ends. A good ride leads uphill - a heathery strip which can be wet. Cross the forest fence and continue uphill. The slope becomes less steep and a little drier, then boulders of granite are scattered everywhere. See how far

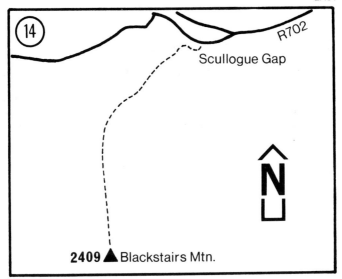

you can get by stepping from one to another! Eventually, the broad top of the mountain is reached - an area of peat hags with a cairn marking the summit.

Alternatives:
An ascent can be made from a gap to the south-west of the summit, using a track from either side of the mountain. If you've climbed Mount Leinster from Kildavin, then descended to Scullogue Gap to climb Blackstairs Mountain, then you might as well complete the traverse of the whole range. The walk can be continued over the lower, heathery hills running southwards, until forestry roads are followed to a minor road network near Drummin. You'll appreciate that there is more to the Blackstairs than the two summits listed.

SOUTH

26 Mountains - 7 Walks

When I write about mountains in the south of Ireland, I mean those mountains clustered around South Tipperary and adjoining counties. Three ranges of mountains and a couple of solitary summits rise from the plains: Slievenamon, the Comeragh Mountains, the Knockmealdown Mountains, the Galty Mountains and Keeper Hill. In very basic terms, the mountains are generally formed of Old Red Sandstone strata - vast thicknesses of sandstones, gritstones and conglomerates. In places there are older slates exposed, while the plains are largely limestone. Despite their close proximity and geological affinities, there is little physical similarity between these ranges.

Slievenamon is a solitary brooding mountain shrouded in ancient legends. Women raced up its slopes for the love of Finn MacCumhail - and you can race to the summit on a broad track. The Comeragh Mountains vary from a sharp, rocky ridge to a broad, boggy plateau. There is a reasonably good access from the signposted Comeragh Drive, but it must be admitted that the best scenery is anywhere but on the summits. The heathery ridge of the shapely Knockmealdown Mountains offers dry walking underfoot, tracing the remains of an old boundary wall and ditch. Again, there is good road access - usually from the Vee Gap, though there are other high-level roads.

The lofty Galty Mountains have forested flanks and the summits all seem rather distant from the roads circling the range. The full traverse of the range is a classic walk and a serious undertaking. There is much heather, bog and steep slopes, but the effort is well worth it and Galtymore is a splendid viewpoint. The bulk of Keeper Hill might be noticed far away - a solitary summit not easily assigned to any other area. It rises above a group of forested hills near the city of Limerick.

PADDY'S WAY - SOUTH

I climbed Slievenamon in continual rain and, thinking ahead, abandoned my plans to visit the Comeragh Mountains next. Instead, I based myself at Lismore Youth Hostel and enjoyed the drier walking offered along the heathery ridge of the Knockmealdown Mountains. The weather soon

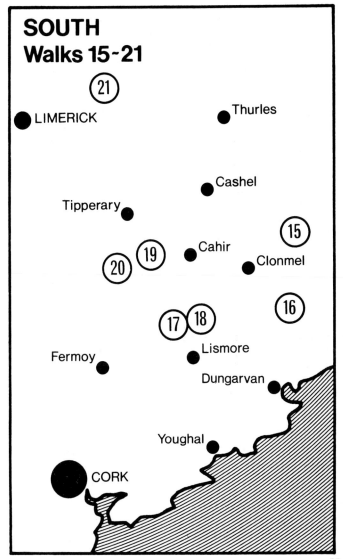

SOUTH
Walks 15-21

㉑

● LIMERICK

● Thurles

● Cashel

Tipperary ●

⑮

⑳ ⑲ ● Cahir

● Clonmel

⑯

⑰ ⑱

Fermoy ●

● Lismore

Dungarvan ●

Youghal ●

● CORK

cleared up and I headed back to the Comeragh Mountains. I started walking fairly late in the day, so couldn't hope to complete the full traverse of the range in a day. I pitched my tent on The Gap and a night of screaming gales almost flattened it. I survived to complete the walk, then moved on to Ballydavid Wood Youth Hostel in the Glen of Aherlow.

Early on a blustery morning, I climbed up through forests and followed the broad crest of the Galty Mountains. The wind was very strong and piercingly cold. I had to shelter from it on Greenane. I hadn't really decided where I was going to spend the night, but had originally hoped to camp on the main ridge. In deference to the weather, I went down to the Mountain Lodge Youth Hostel. Most unusually for me, I took a day off - which indicates how tired I must have been at this stage. When I finally scaled Galtymore, there was a considerable snow cover - spring was indeed late! I pressed onwards to complete the whole range, got a lift to Cork city where I stopped in the youth hostel, then continued towards the south-west.

WALK 15:

Summit:	Slievenamon 2,368ft (720m) S 297307
Character:	A solitary, pudding-like mountain with an easy ascent.
Distance:	3 miles (5 kilometres).
Maps:	1:50,000 Sheets 67 & 75. Half Inch Sheet 18.
Start/Finish:	Kilcash.
Getting There:	Kilcash lies on a minor road off the main N76 road between Clonmel and Callan.

THE ROUTE

Slievenamon (sliabh na mbán = mountain of the women)
From Kilcash, go steeply uphill by road to leave the village, then turn left at a signpost for Slievenamon. Turn right by road, continuing uphill, then take the first track on the left which has no gates. Follow this track, which becomes a fine grassy line between walls. Go through a gate and stay on the most obvious stony track on the open mountainside. As the track climbs, it is flanked by heather and never strays far from a nearby forest

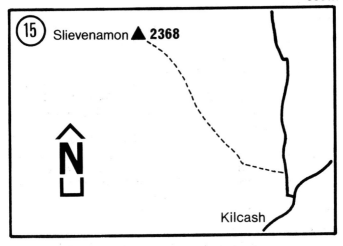

⑮ Slievenamon ▲ 2368

↑ N ⎵

Kilcash

fence. Later, it runs free across broad, heathery slopes to reach the top of the mountain. The summit is marked by a trig point and large cairn. As this is a solitary summit, views in all directions are very good. Most days feature views of the Galtys, Knockmealdowns and Comeraghs, while the Blackstairs and Wicklow Mountains might feature distantly. Other notable heights might be seen across the plains on very clear days.

Alternatives:
Any other route up Slievenamon is of course more difficult than the clear track described. The mountain is really too remote to consider linking with any other group, though its nearest neighbours are the Comeraghs. In between Slievenamon and the Comeraghs is the Munster Way, which links with the South Leinster Way, offering a route to the distant Blackstairs Mountains for long distance walkers.

WALK 16:

Summits:	Knocksheegowna	2,181ft (663m)	S 278167
	Knockanaffrin	2,478ft (754m)	S 285153
	Fauscoum North Top	2,500ft (760m)	S 311121
	Fauscoum	2,597ft (790m)	S 318105
	Coumalocha	2,444ft (743m)	S 295098
	Seefin	2,387ft (726m)	S 274069
	Coumaraglin-mountain	2,000ft (610m)	S 280041

Character:	Seven summits ranging from sharp peaks to broad bogs. A long, hard walk through the Comeragh Mountains links the summits. Not recommended in mist or after days of rain.
Distance:	15 miles (24 kilometres).
Maps:	1:50,000 Sheet 75. Half Inch Sheet 22. 1:25,000 Sheet Comeragh Mountains (not an OS publication)
Start:	Glenpatrick.
Finish:	Dalligan Bridge.
Getting There:	Glenpatrick and Dalligan Bridge are on the northern and southern parts of the scenic, signposted Comeragh Drive, which can be joined near Clonmel or Dungarvan.

THE ROUTE

Knocksheegowna (cnoc sídh gamhna = hill of the fairy calves)
Start from the crossroads at Glenpatrick, taking a good track southwards to reach the edge of a forest. Walk uphill through a couple of fields, keeping close to the edge of the forest, then climb steeply up a grassy slope to reach the main ridge above. Turn left and walk up to a series of prominent rocky outcrops. One of these sharp peaks almost hides the summit trig point from view.

Knockanaffrin (cnoc an aiffrin = hill of the mass)
Walk along the sharp, rocky ridge, descending to a gap of grass and boulders. Climb steeply uphill to reach a fine, rocky ridge and follow this to reach the summit cairn. Views from the top of Knockanaffrin take in the desolate Comeragh plateau, the Knockmealdowns, Galtys,

Slievenamon and distant Blackstairs Mountains.

Fauscoum North Top
Walk along the serrated crest of Knockanaffrin, passing rocky peaks and outcrops. The ground starts to fall more steeply and care is needed in areas of rock and deep heather. A gap is reached - simply called The Gap - which has wooden marker posts to show you quick exits from these mountains. Straight ahead, a steep slope rises from The Gap and seems to end in a formidable cliff. The cliff can be outflanked on either side, though experienced scramblers might like to attempt some of its gullies and ledges. Either way, the higher ground above the cliff is set at a gentler gradient. Keep going uphill across a broad, stony area and choose any likely looking point to call the summit.

Fauscoum (fásachcúm = wild hollow)
Descend a stony slope from the North Top, enjoying the last firm footing before reaching a broad, boggy gap. This is difficult to cross and diversions will need to be made around several soft patches. Look ahead to locate a stony channel, which offers the best means of progress uphill. Eventually, there seems to be no option but a boggy thrash up the final gentle slope. The summit area is broad and wet, but not too boggy, and there is a cairn. Immediate views are desolate, but the distant vista is good. Unfortunately, there is no way of appreciating the splendid Coumshingaun - a vast hollow which falls away from the summit of Fauscoum.

Coumalocha (cúm an locha = hollow of the lake)
I've had a long, hard look at the middle part of the Comeragh plateau, as well as the satellites of Fauscoum, and have determined that not every hump and bump should be treated as a separate summit. Walk north-westwards from Fauscoum to cross a broad and boggy gap. Aim for a distant moorland hump which is one of those failing to achieve the status of a separate summit. Once on this gentle rise, turn and walk south-westwards across another boggy gap. A gentle climb over sodden grass leads to a broad area of moorland. There is nothing to mark the actual summit, so scout around for the highest part.

Seefin (suí Finn = seat of Finn)
Walk south-westwards from the broad summit of Coumalocha, eventually crossing a narrow neck of moorland supported by steep cliffs plunging into nearby coums. If you think the slight rise of Coumfea ranks as a separate summit, which I don't, then you can include it with a short

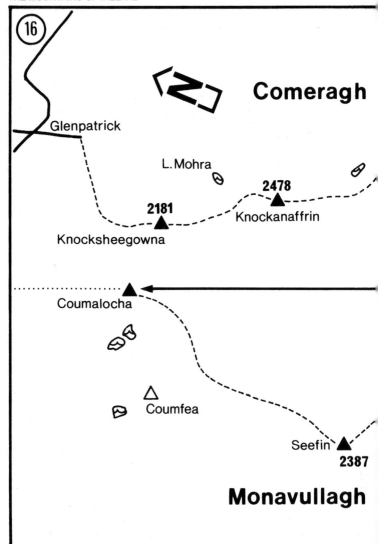

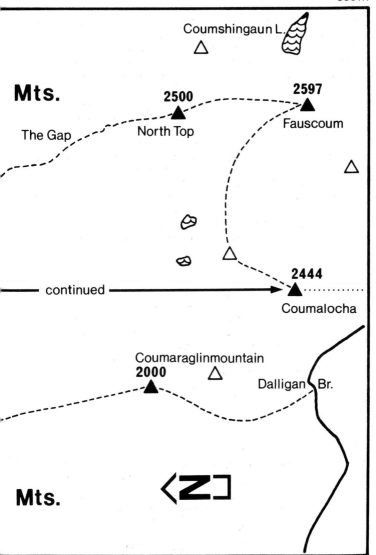

Coumshingaun L.

Mts.

The Gap

2500
▲
North Top

2597
▲
Fauscoum

continued ⟶

2444
▲
Coumalocha

Coumaraglinmountain
2000
▲

Dalligan Br.

Mts.

61

diversion. Otherwise, maintain a course south-westwards, crossing areas of bog and tussocky grass while negotiating a broad gap. A gentle climb on much firmer ground leads to the top of Seefin. There is a fallen trig point on the summit, an old cairn and an ugly hut. If a rapid descent is needed, simply follow a broad track down towards Kilbrien.

Coumaraglinmountain (cúm aragail = hollow of the ledge)
A fence leads away from the summit of Seefin, later running down a steep, stony slope to reach Barnamaddra Gap. There is a white-painted standing stone on the gap, near a drystone sheepfold. Continue to follow the fence, which climbs a grassy slope to reach a rather wet summit. There is nothing to mark the highest point, though a couple of huts arrayed in aerials stand nearby.

In mist, it's best to stay close to the fence and later turn right and follow the edge of a forest down to the road. In clear weather, walk gradually away from the fence, keeping well to the right of the forest to descend to a minor road. The road is part of the Comeragh Drive and the walk can be ended close to the forest at Dalligan Bridge.

Alternatives:
This long walk can be split into sections by using the following access paths and tracks. First: the waymarked path running across The Gap offers access to and from the Knockanaffrin ridge. Second: Seefin can be reached via a broad, bulldozed track from near Kilbrien. Finally: there is a path to Coumshingaun, which offers perhaps the most scenic approach to any walk in the Comeragh Mountains, and can be used to gain the summit of Fauscoum. There's no doubting that these mountains are forbiddingly boggy and mostly quite featureless, but the surrounding coums are splendid and well worth discovering.

WALK 17:

Summits:	Knockaunabulloga	2,069ft (629m)	S 020101
	Knockshanahullion	2,153ft (655m)	R 999104
Character:	Two mountain summits to the west of the Vee Gap which can be visited by a fairly simple walk.		
Distance:	6 miles (10 kilometres).		
Maps:	1:50,000 Sheet 74. Half Inch Sheet 22.		

Looking along the Galty ridge from Temple Hill (Walk 20)
The Priest's Leap, on the way to Knockboy (Walk 26)

Knockowen rises above the rock-bound Healy Pass (Walk 28)
Mullaghanattin - the highest of the mountains around The Pocket
(Walk 35)

Start/Finish: The Vee Gap.

Getting There: The Vee Gap can be reached via the R668 road from
Lismore or Cahir, or the R669 road from Cappoquin.

THE ROUTE

Knockaunabulloga (cnocán na mbulog = little hill of the bullocks)
There is a car park on top of the Vee Gap, close to a grotto. Simply head
westwards, tracing an overgrown bank and ditch steeply uphill. This can
be a bit difficult in places, as there is heather and stunted rhododendrons
on the lower slopes. The higher parts are less lushly vegetated and run
at a gentler angle. Note that the bank dwindles in size and turns sharply
left before reaching the summit of Knockaunabulloga. Follow instead a
vague groove through the heather to reach an outcrop of rock. The
outcrop has been broken into blocks to make a small cairn to mark the
summit.

Knockshanahullion (cnoc sean na h-uillinn = hill of the old elbow)
Walk southwards down a heathery slope to pick up the line of the
banking which was being followed earlier. This vague boundary is now
marked by a peaty scrape, but as it swings westwards to cross a wide
gap it becomes rather like a stony path in appearance. There is nothing
to show the way up Knockshanahullion, so just walk straight uphill. The
slope levels out and there are a few boulders among the heather. A trig
point stands on the summit, plus an enormous burial cairn which has
been used to construct smaller cairns and a shelter. Good views reach
across a wide vale to the Galty Mountains. Walk back along the
boundary line to return to the Vee Gap.

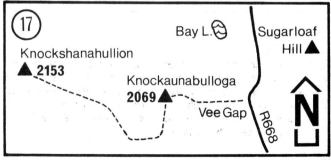

Alternatives:

It's also possible to descend northwards from Knockshanahullion, turning right to follow the edge of some forestry plantations. This allows a peep into some small valleys on the way back to the Vee Gap. For a longer walk, start on the minor road to the west of Knockshanahullion, then walk eastwards over these two summits. The walk can then be continued across the Vee Gap and along all the other Knockmealdown summits as described in Walk 18.

WALK 18:

Summits:	Sugarloaf Hill	2,144ft (652m)	S 039107
	Knockmoylan	2,521ft (767m)	S 058094
	Knockmealdown	2,609ft (793m)	S 058085
	Knocknagnauv	2,152ft (654m)	S 082084
	Knocknafallia	2,199ft (668m)	S 095075

Character: Five heathery mountains often peppered with boulders. The walk traces a low, stony embankment over most of them.

Distance: 8 miles (13 kilometres).

Maps: 1:50,000 Sheet 74. Half Inch Sheet 22.

Start: The Vee Gap.

Finish: Glennafallia.

Getting There: The Vee Gap can be reached via the R668 road from Lismore or Cahir, or the R669 road from Cappoquin. Glennafallia is on a minor road between Cappoquin and Newcastle.

THE ROUTE

Sugarloaf Hill

Head eastwards from the Vee Gap, following a prominent drystone embankment steeply uphill. The slopes of Sugarloaf Hill are stony and heathery, but there is a fairly well trodden path. At the end of the ascent, the embankment turns sharply right, but we must head to the left first to reach the nearby summit of Sugarloaf Hill. There is a cairn and a good view across to the Galty Mountains.

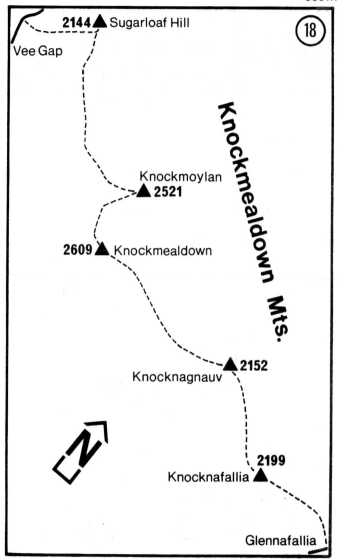

2144 ▲ Sugarloaf Hill

Vee Gap

Knockmoylan
▲ 2521

2609 ▲ Knockmealdown

Knockmealdown Mts.

▲ 2152
Knocknagnauv

N

2199
Knocknafallia ▲

Glennafallia

Knockmoylan (cnoc maolán = little bald hill)
Return to the stony embankment and follow it away from the summit of
Sugarloaf Hill. It runs downhill to cross a broad gap, then climbs uphill.
Knockmoylan isn't actually on the line of the embankment, so you'll need
to branch away to the left, crossing a shallow gap to reach it. There is
a vague path which goes most of the way across the gap, but is quickly
lost on the rocky hump of Knockmoylan. Climb up to the summit, which
is marked with a cairn.

Knockmealdown (cnoc maol donn = bald brown hill)
Another vague path can be followed back across the gap from
Knockmoylan towards the stony embankment. Once the embankment
is reached, continue to follow it uphill to reach the summit of
Knockmealdown. There is a trig point on top, as well as the ruins of a hut
which once stood nearby. This is the highest point in Co Waterford.
Views lead in from the coast to pass the Comeragh Mountains and
Slievenamon, before tracking round to the Galty Mountains.

Knocknagnauv (cnoc na gcnámh = hill of the bones)
Follow the stony bank steeply downhill on the heathery slopes of
Knockmealdown. The bank levels out on a wide, heathery gap, then
later becomes only a vague mound. A path runs alongside it. The bank
increases in size for the ascent of Knocknagnauv and can be followed
with confidence all the way to the summit. There are three gentle
swellings on the top of the mountain - the middle one being the highest.

Knocknafallia (cnoc na fallaí = hill of the walls)
The banking no longer offers a sure guide along the Knockmealdown
Mountains as it leads straight from Knocknagnauv to Knockmeal, by-
passing the summit of Knocknafallia. There are no paths over
Knocknafallia, so walk up the stony and heathery slopes to reach the
broad top of the mountain. A cairn will be passed, but this isn't on the
highest point. Locate another cairn which marks the summit and has
been built into a shelter overlooking Mount Melleray Monastery.

Descend eastwards down a very steep slope, towards a forest
rather than the next gap along the ridge. A wide track can be found
leading into the forest and this can be followed quickly down to a minor
road at Glennafallia. It's useful if you can be picked up at this point. If you
need to retrace your steps to the Vee Gap, then it's best to do it from the
summit of Knocknafallia.

Alternatives:
The arrangement of summits along the Knockmealdown Mountains doesn't really allow for circular walks. However, if you do wish to enjoy a long circular walk, then you could return to the Vee Gap by following the waymarked Munster Way, though this lies some distance to the north of the mountains. Shorter walks are possible by picking off odd summits from the Vee Gap and Glennafallia, without completing the whole ridge walk. It's also possible to extend the ridge walk by combining Walk 17 with Walk 18.

WALK 19:

Summits:	Laghtshanaquilla	2,010ft (611m)	R 953248
	Greenane	2,639ft (803m)	R 925239
	O'Loughnan's Castle	2,500ft (760m)	R 910240
	Binnia	2,109ft (641m)	R 894261

Character: The four eastern summits of the Galty Mountains form a fine circuit, but this is a long, hard walk with a difficult ascent on forested moorland slopes.

Distance: 12 miles (20 kilometres).

Maps: 1:50,000 Sheet 74. Half Inch Sheets 18 & 22.

Start: Ballydavid Wood Youth Hostel.

Finish: Glencoshabinnia.

Getting There: The start and finish are in the Glen of Aherlow, which can be reached via minor roads from Cahir or Tipperary. The youth hostel is signposted.

THE ROUTE

Laghtshanaquilla (leac sean na coille = rock of the old cock)
After reaching Ballydavid Wood Youth Hostel on a narrow road, follow a track further into the forest, then turn left to go up a grassy ride. This becomes quite tight, but cuts a loop from the track. Turn left along the next section of track, then head off to the right up another ride. This eventually reaches a small, clear area overlooking a stream. Branch to the right and walk up a rough, overgrown ride to reach another track. Cross straight over this last track and forge up a heathery slope which

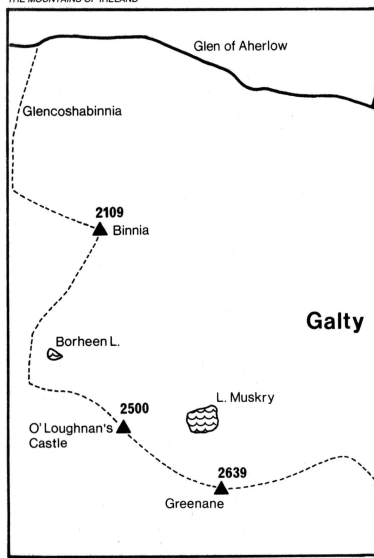

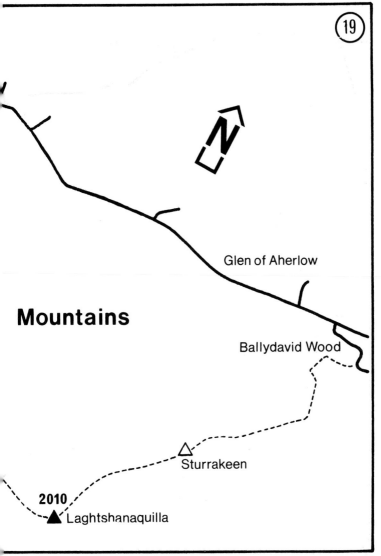

N

Glen of Aherlow

Mountains

Ballydavid Wood

△ Sturrakeen

2010
▲ Laghtshanaquilla

Looking from Greenane, across Lough Muskry to Galtymore

has been planted with small trees. Cross the forest fence on Sturrakeen and continue over a false summit before reaching Laghtshanaquilla. The summit is heathery, bouldery and marked with a cairn.

Greenane (grianán = sunny place)
Follow a low, stone bank down from Laghtshanaquilla and continue along this line to cross a peaty gap. Traces of an old boundary ditch are easily lost among peat hags, but a few small cairns show the way uphill. Grass takes over from heather on the ascent and the walking becomes

70

easier. As the shoulder of Greenane is mounted there is a large shelter cairn from which there is a good view across to Galtymore. The summit of Greenane is marked by a squat trig point.

O'Loughnan's Castle:

Go down from Greenane, walking eastwards to cross a gap. There is a minor bump of moorland to be crossed, but nothing which would count as a separate summit, then a descent to another gap. This is where O'Loughnan's Castle really is - a large blocky outcrop of rock sitting on the gap. In some nearby views it really does look like a castle, but is entirely natural. I've borrowed its name to tag onto the next rise on the broad, moorland crest. There are a few metal fenceposts crossing this bleak bulge, but nothing to mark the actual summit.

Binnia (binn = mountain)

On the descent from the broad moor, the twin peaks of Galtybeg and Galtymore loom large, but we must watch where we are planting our feet as there is some bog to negotiate. Go down to a gap, then exit to the right, rather than climb Galtybeg. There is a path across the steep, northern slopes of Galtybeg, overlooking Borheen Lough. Although the slopes are very steep, the path is gently graded and simply heads across to a grassy spur which runs down to a lower gap. An overgrown stone bank can be found part-way up the slopes of Binnia. Follow this as far as it goes, then keep going steeply uphill to reach a minor rise at the top of the slope. By walking further along the crest of the mountain, the summit will be reached, which is simply marked by a rock outcrop.

A steep descent can be made westwards into Glencoshabinnia, then by turning right a farm access track can be followed through a forestry plantation to reach a minor road. If someone can come and collect you at this point, then the walk is over. If you have to return to Ballydavid Wood, then miles of tarmac bashing remain. You could, with care, try and link various forest tracks to return to the youth hostel.

Alternatives:

This walk can be combined with Walk 20 to enable all the summits in the Galty Mountains to be covered together. However, this would be a very long and hard walk, embracing more than even the classic Galty Ridge Walk attempts to do. It's also possible to amend the walk by heading down to the Mountain Lodge Youth Hostel, rather than returning to Ballydavid Wood Youth Hostel. This would leave you in a good position for completing the remaining summits in the Galty Mountains.

WALK 20:

Summits:	Galtybeg	2,600ft (790m)	R 890240
	Galtymore	3,018ft (918m)	R 879237
	Monabrack	2,000ft (610m)	R 861219
	Lyracappul	2,712ft (825m)	R 846232
	Knockaterriff	2,287ft (695m)	R 849216
	Temple Hill	2,579ft (784m)	R 834219

Character:	Six summits on the western side of the Galty Mountains. Two of these lie significantly off the main ridge, so the route involves a certain amount of backtracking and is consequently quite long and hard.
Distance:	18 miles (29 kilometres).
Maps:	1:50,000 Sheet 74. Half Inch Sheet 22.
Start:	Skeheenaranky.
Finish:	Castlequarter.
Getting There:	Skeheenaranky is on the main N8 road between Cahir and Mitchelstown. Castlequarter is off the main road near Kilbeheny.

THE ROUTE

Galtybeg (sliabh coillte beag = little wooded mountain)
The Black Road is one of the most direct mountain access roads in Ireland, but it can be awkward to locate. It rises between Skeheenaranky and the entrance to Glengarra Wood, but isn't signposted. There is a disused pub on the corner where the Black Road leaves the main N8 road. The minor road climbs gradually uphill, then becomes more roughly surfaced as it crosses high moorlands. After climbing the flanks of Knockeenatoung, this clear track seems set to reach the top of Galtybeg. However, it comes to an end just short of the final steep slopes. Walkers cross a few old turf cuttings, then mount the final steep slopes by their own routes. Grass and heather are crossed at first, then the upper part of the mountain is bouldery. There is a fine, narrow, rocky ridge leading to the summit cairn.

Galtymore (sliabh coillte mór = big wooded mountain)
Head straight for Galtymore, losing height rapidly to descend to a gap overlooking a tiny lough. Avoid a boggy climb from the gap by staying on firmer ground to the right. Walk up steep, almost corrugated ground, which gradually becomes rockier. As the ground begins to level out, huge blocks of conglomerate rock litter the top of the mountain. There is a broken trig point on the summit, a cairn and a nearby white metal cross. This is the highest point in both Co Tipperary and Co Limerick. As the Galty Mountains rise steeply from the surrounding plains, the panoramic view is splendid. Nearby are the Knockmealdowns, Comeraghs and Slievenamon, while on the clearest days the view may stretch from the Wicklow Mountains to the Mountains of Kerry.

Monabrack (móin na bhráca = speckled bog)
Walk along Galtymore's broad summit ridge to reach a large cairn poised above a steep slope. Go down the slope to reach the end of a stout wall. Follow this wall faithfully - it offers a sure guide in mist. One section has been levelled - presumably trundled down a steep slope into a lough below. The wall starts to climb from a gap and crosses the minor summit of Slievecushnabinnia. When the wall runs down to a slight gap, branch left away from it to contour around the southern slopes of Carrignabinnia. Head down a grassy spur, negotiating old turf cuttings while crossing a boggy gap. Walk straight up the slopes of Monabrack. There is a vague path which can be followed in spite of the rugged terrain. A level, heathery summit is marked with a small cairn. Good views look back to the main ridge of the Galty Mountains.

Lyracappul
Retrace steps across the boggy gap, crossing the old turf cuttings as before, then climb the grassy spur to regain the main Galty ridge. As the ground levels out the wall will be reached and a left turn takes walkers over the minor summit of Carrignabinnia. Continue across a slight gap, then climb up to the shapely peak of Lyracappul, where the wall ends quite suddenly.

Knockaterriff (cnoc na dtarbh = hill of the bull)
Descend roughly southwards on the steep and rugged slopes of Lyracappul. There is no path, but a couple of old fenceposts might be noticed. After negotiating some bouldery areas, a wide, boggy gap has to be crossed. A minor summit of heather and grass gives way to another

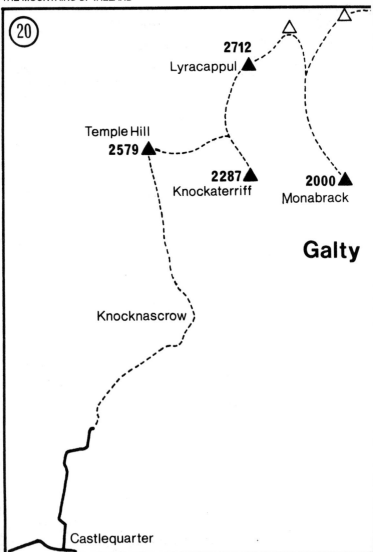

20

2712
Lyracappul ▲

Temple Hill
2579 ▲

2287 ▲
Knockaterriff

2000 ▲
Monabrack

Galty

Knocknascrow

Castlequarter

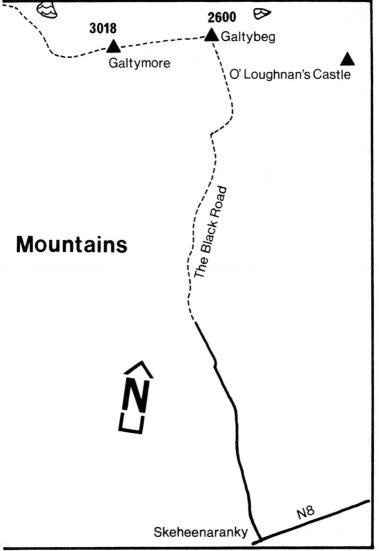

3018
Galtymore

2600 ▲ Galtybeg

▲ O' Loughnan's Castle

Mountains

The Black Road

N̂

N8

Skeheenaranky

The snowy summit of Galtymore, high above the plains

boggy gap. A short ascent leads to the small summit cairn on Knockaterriff.

Temple Hill

Retrace steps to the last boggy gap and climb the minor rise beyond. Turn left and descend to yet another boggy gap - lower than the previous ones. There are a few more old fenceposts which might be noticed along this line. There is also a grassy strip up the flank of Temple Hill which offers easy walking. The ascent leads to a rash of boulders and a fairly level area of these is crowned with a huge summit cairn. The cairn has been fashioned into a shelter and there is also a trig point. Good views look back along the Galty ridge.

Descend via the broad, stony southern ridge of Temple Hill to pick up a stony track. Be careful not to be drawn along the bulldozed track at the edge of a forest, though you could in fact make a descent that way. The high track varies from being firm and stony to being a boggy groove. There are other paths and tracks on this high moorland, but try and stay on the clearest one. It later follows the line of a fence as it descends, then becomes enclosed before reaching a farm. The farm access road leads down to a minor road at Castlequarter. If you can be picked up here, you can save yourself the walk back along the main N8 road from Kilbeheny to the Black Road, which isn't included in the distance quoted.

Alternatives:

This walk can be split into separate walks. For instance, the two Galtys can be tackled together in a fairly simple walk from the end of the Black Road. Other summits could be covered in a circuit from Monabrack Wood, while Temple Hill could be climbed purely for its own sake. It's also possible to link this walk with Walk 19 to cover all the Galty Mountains in a long, hard walk. This would be rather tougher than even the classic Galty Ridge Walk, so the suggestion is reserved for hardy mountain walkers.

WALK 21:

Summit:	Keeper Hill	2,279ft (692m)	R 824666

Character:	An isolated mountain in a forested range of hills which can be climbed on a good, clear, well-graded track.
Distance:	6 miles (10 kilometres).
Maps:	1:50,000 Sheet 59. Half Inch Sheet 18.
Start/Finish:	Doonane Wood car park.
Getting There:	Doonane Wood is east of the city of Limerick and can be reached after passing through Newport.

THE ROUTE

Keeper Hill

Before leaving the car park in Doonane Wood, study the mapboard which shows the layout of various roads, tracks and trails in the Silvermine and Slievefelim Mountains. Follow a sparse series of white waymark arrows, which are intended to lead walkers over to the Ballyhourigan Valley. These arrows should be used to indicate your choice of tracks only as far as a wide, forested gap planted with young trees. At this point, turn right to follow another track which contours around the unplanted slopes of Keeper Hill. A left turn later leads along a track which climbs the heathery upper slopes of the mountain. There is a summit trig point and cairn alongside a series of masts. As Keeper Hill is so isolated, views of other mountain groups will be both rare and distant, but the expanse of lower hills in view is great. You can either

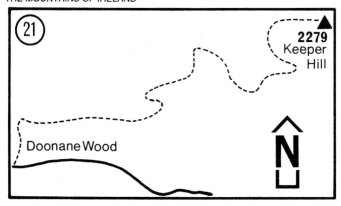

retrace your steps to Doonane Wood, or go back via the Ballyhourigan Valley by following waymarks.

Alternatives:
Any other ascent of Keeper Hill is over rough ground, particularly a direct ascent from the northern side of the mountain.

SOUTH-WEST

81 Mountains - 26 Walks

The south-west of Ireland is crowded with mountains. They rise up in no particular order in West Cork, then align themselves along the Beara peninsula. Next door is the Iveragh peninsula, containing Ireland's highest mountains and crowned by Carrauntoohil. A handful of the summits are easily reached on good paths, but most of them require considerable effort to reach. Moving on, the Dingle peninsula is best known for Brandon Mountain, though there are several other mountains to visit. To oversimplify the geology, these mountains are almost all composed of Old Red Sandstone. However, the thick beds of sandstones, gritstones and conglomerates have been crumpled into a highly contorted and complex form. Sharp peaks and ridges are common, with deep hollows filled with loughs and rugged slopes leading down to boggy, bouldery glens.

Tourism in the south-west is often geared to exploiting the scenic charms of the area, but the mountains remain inviolate. Those mountains closest to Killarney are included in the Killarney National Park. The scenic Ring of Kerry tour allows a view of all the mountain ranges on the Iveragh peninsula, while the Ring of Beara tour does the same on the Beara peninsula. Hopefully, there will never be a Ring of Dingle tour, which would involve cutting a new road over Brandon Mountain. None of the mountains in the south-west could really be said to be remote, but they are mostly rugged, boggy and prone to sudden changes in the weather.

Walkers have for a long time tackled the problems of Macgillycuddys Reeks, or scaled the likes of Carrauntoohil and Brandon Mountain. Devout walkers may have followed the Stations of the Cross up Knocknadobar. In some places, you could meet groups of walkers, but for the most part you'd not meet anyone. The Kerry Way - a long distance walkers' alternative to the Ring of Kerry - can be used to reach some of the mountains, as can the waymarked Dingle Way. Experienced mountain walkers might prefer to combine some of the walks to create long, high-level expeditions. I offer a few pointers in this respect.

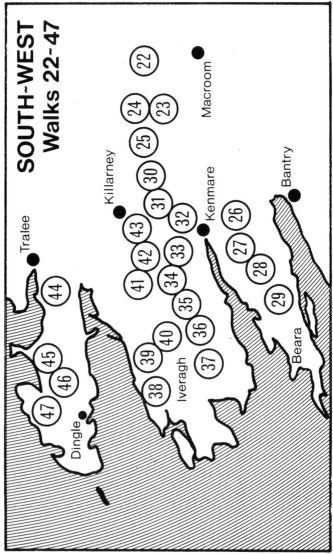

PADDY'S WAY - SOUTH-WEST

My springtime saunter through the mountains of Ireland took me through West Cork in deteriorating weather. I got up a couple of mountains - even spending the night on one - but finally had to retire to Killarney Youth Hostel to get dried. I walked into the Gap of Dunloe, only to be beaten back by wind and rain. I dried off again, then scaled Purple Mountain with an American walker. I covered the summits along the ridge of Macgillycuddys Reeks on one foul day, then took a day off to look around the Killarney National Park. When the weather cleared, I climbed Carrauntoohil as part of the Coomloughra Horseshoe, then moved my base to Loo Bridge Youth Hostel. I managed to cover The Paps and Mangerton Mountain before I had to break my mountain journey for a while.

It was early summer when I returned to walk the Kerry Way. From time to time I broke off from the route and covered all the mountains on the Iveragh peninsula. Several days were spent in the company of a Dutch walker. I stayed nowhere more than a couple of nights and alternated between An Oige Youth Hostels and Independent Hostels. One miserable night was spent in my tent high on the mountains above Sneem, in the pouring rain.

When I'd completed the Kerry Way I walked over all the mountains of the Beara peninsula. For this rugged series of mountains, I based myself first at Glanmore Lake Youth Hostel, then moved to the Independent Hostel at Bonane. After that, I headed straight for the Dingle Peninsula and embarked on a walk around the Dingle Way. I broke off the route from time to time to climb all the mountains on the Dingle peninsula. I stayed in Independent Hostels, except for a memorable night in a tent on Brandon Mountain - the only time the cloud lifted from its summit in four weeks!

When I left the south-west I climbed Keeper Hill after passing through Limerick. This outlying mountain has been listed earlier in this guide, but I found it convenient to include it after my tour of the south-west. I was leaving the mountains for a while, but reflected that I had spent nearly half of my total time allowance on the mountains of the south-west. There's certainly a lot of rough country to cover in that corner of Ireland.

WALK 22:

Summit:	Musheramore	2,118ft (644m)	W 328850

Character: A fairly easy ascent of a solitary summit in West Cork.

Distance: 1 mile (1½ kilometres).

Maps: 1:50,000 Sheet 79. Half Inch Sheet 21.

Start/Finish: On the western side of Musheramore.

Getting There: The western side of Musheramore can be reached by negotiating a network of minor roads between Millstreet and Macroom.

THE ROUTE

Musheramore

The hardest part of this walk probably lies in navigating to the junction of minor roads on the western side of Musheramore. Signposts for Knocknakilla Stone Circle will get you part of the way. From the road junction, a fence runs straight uphill and offers a sure guide all the way from the road to the summit. The walk starts with tussocky grass and boulders, which is quickly replaced with heather. The final stretch to the summit reveals the trig point near to the fence, a cairn to the left and a metal cross to the right.

Alternatives:

Any other approach would be either on forested slopes or lengthy moorland slopes. I once linked Musheramore to its nearest neighbour - Mullaghanish - and do not particularly recommend that exercise to readers of this guide.

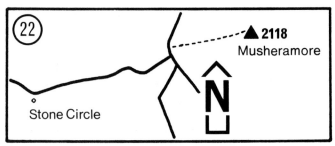

WALK 23:

Summit:	Mullaghanish 2,133ft (649m) W 215817
Character:	A simple road-walk up to a summit bearing a TV mast.
Distance:	2 miles (3 kilometres).
Maps:	1:50,000 Sheet 79. Half Inch Sheet 21.
Start/Finish:	On a minor road north of Ballyvourney.
Getting There:	Ballyvourney is on the main N22 road between Macroom and Killarney. Mullaghanish is signposted from there.

THE ROUTE

Mullaghanish (mullach an ais = summit of the back)
Mullaghanish is signposted from Ballyvourney, making navigation to the foot of this mountain easy. Cars are usually barred from making the ascent of the mountain by a pair of locked gates. The road zig-zags up enclosed grassy slopes, then heads up heathery slopes to reach the summit. There is a tall TV mast which is a landmark for miles around and views look over the mountains of West Cork and Kerry, featuring some rugged heights.

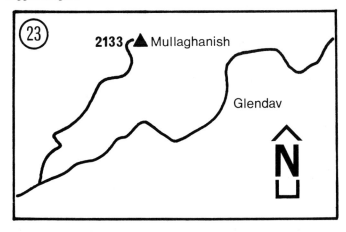

Alternatives:
Any other approach to this summit is hard work. Most of the slopes are forested, while broad, boggy moorlands are a feature of the upper ground. Hardy walkers might consider walking towards Caherbarnagh and The Paps, but it's all tough country.

WALK 24:

Summit:	Caherbarnagh	2,239ft (681m) W 191871
Character:	A solitary summit surrounded by stern moorlands.	
Distance:	5 miles (8 kilometres).	
Maps:	1:50,000 Sheet 79. Half Inch Sheet 21.	
Start/Finish:	Near the head of the Clydagh Valley.	
Getting There:	The Clydagh Valley can be reached via a minor road from the main N22 road between Ballyvourney and Killarney.	

THE ROUTE

Caherbarnagh (cathair bearna = fort of the pass)
The walk starts from a solitary farm near the head of the Clydagh Valley. Walk up a tributary stream from the main Clydagh River, then later cut off to the right to climb the broad slopes of Caherbarnagh. Heather and tussocky grass make this a difficult ascent, and there are no paths to follow. As height is gained, look out for a series of old fenceposts. These are useful aids to navigation in mist as they lead all the way to the summit. There is a trig point in this desolate area. There are also two minor bumps to the north-west and north-east. I don't consider these to be separate summits, but some walkers may feel that after the effort of getting here at all, they are entitled to a greater reward! If you want them, there they are, otherwise walk back down into the Clydagh Valley.

Alternatives:
This walk, although short, is hard enough. The surrounding moors are often quite difficult to cross. If you really wanted to, you could reach either The Paps or Mullaghanish by keeping to the rugged high ground above the Clydagh Valley.

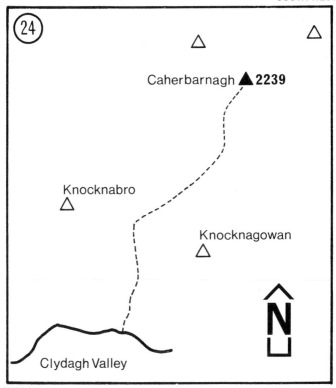

WALK 25:

Summits:	The Paps (East)	2,284ft (694m) W 133855
	The Paps (West)	2,273ft (691m) W 125855
Character:	Two aptly-named summits which are readily distinguished in many views around West Cork and Kerry. An easy walk.	
Distance:	4 miles (6 kilometres).	
Maps:	1:50,000 Sheet 79. Half Inch Sheet 21.	
Start/Finish:	Half way up the Clydagh Valley.	
Getting There:	The Clydagh Valley can be reached via a minor road from the main N22 road between Ballyvourney and Killarney.	

THE ROUTE

The Paps (East) (dá chíoch Dhána = two breasts of Dana)

Start the walk from the Clydagh Valley, using a track between a modern bungalow and some derelict, tin-roofed buildings. The track runs gradually uphill through a great gap in the hills which has been forested. On the highest part of the gap, there is a grassy strip fenced off between two parts of the forestry plantations. Walk up this strip and continue onto the heathery slopes above. Bear a little to the right to pass some ruined drystone structures. Vaguely trodden paths on this rugged slope are soon lost, but the heather becomes shorter and easier to cross as height is gained. The summit cairn is enormous and was obviously constructed to resemble a huge nipple. It has been finished off with a tall, columnar cairn which rather spoils the effect, though this is obviously a later addition.

The Paps (West) (dá chíoch Dhána = two breasts of Dana)

Descend past some small, blade-like outcrops of rock, crossing stony patches to reach a gap. Heather gives way to grass on the gap, but heather rises to the next Pap. Again, there are small, blade-like outcrops of rock. Another nipple-cairn stands on the summit - again spoilt by the addition of a columnar cairn. A trig point also stands alongside. Good views range over the mountains of West Cork and Kerry - we're getting there by degrees! Retrace steps to the Clydagh Valley to end this walk.

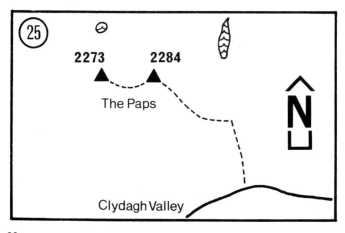

The Paps - looking from one summit to the other

Alternatives:

The Paps can also be climbed from the northern side by following a pilgrim track towards the forested gap. It's also possible to make an ascent from Glenflesk, on the main N22 road, by using a long farm access track which continues towards the Paps. The ascent of The Paps could also be the start of the long and hard walk around the Clydagh Valley, covering miles of tussocky moorlands to reach Caherbarnagh and Mullaghanish.

WALK 26:

Summits:	Knockboy	2,321ft (707m)	W	005620
	Caoinkeen	2,280ft (695m)	W	011646
	Gullaba Hill	2,000ft (610m)	W	001671
	Barrerneen	2,099ft (639m)	V	990660
Character:	Four mountain summits linked on a high-level circuit. Good access tracks, but rough walking on top.			
Distance:	11 miles (18 kilometres).			
Maps:	1:50,000 Sheet 85. Half Inch Sheet 24.			

Start/Finish: Drehideighteragh Bridge.

Getting There: The bridge is reached via minor roads from Bunane, which is on the main N71 road between Glengarriff and Kenmare.

THE ROUTE

Knockboy (cnoc buí = yellow hill)

The road crossing Drehideighteragh Bridge continues across Drehidoughteragh Bridge (if we believe the spellings on the map, which indicates a change of only two letters!). A stony track runs uphill from a farm, offering a clear line to the top of a pass called the Priest's Leap. A metal cross marks the spot where a Jesuit priest on horseback, being hotly pursued, spurred his horse to leap almost to Bantry! Turn left to leave the highest part of the track at some turf cuttings. Wander across rugged moorland slopes to reach the hidden pool of Lough Boy. A fence runs uphill from the little lough, offering a sure guide almost to the summit of Knockboy. The tough vegetation encountered on the ascent becomes shorter on top and a trig point marks the summit. Views take in the mountains of West Cork and Kerry, including a stretch of Bantry Bay. Knockboy is the highest point in Co Cork.

Caoinkeen

Walk roughly northwards from Knockboy, passing small rocky outcrops and boggy patches on the rugged descent. A broad gap is crossed, and although the walking becomes easier, the ground is still quite boggy. In mist, this could be an awkward place to cross, with little Lough Nambrackdarrig being the only aid to navigation. A heathery slope leads onto Caoinkeen, whose summit is marked with a cairn perched above a cliff.

Gullaba Hill (guala bó = shoulder of the cow)

Head north-westwards from the summit of Caoinkeen, taking care to pass safely between two cliff-lines on the descent. The way down to a broad gap is steep and bouldery, becoming boggier later. A fence is joined on the gap and this can be followed straight uphill until it suddenly turns left. At this point, we must turn right, away from the fence, to cross a wide and boggy gap. A short ascent leads to the end of a fence, which serves to mark this summit. The name Gullaba Hill has been borrowed

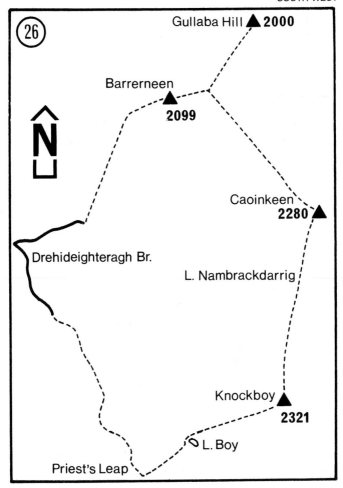

from a minor summit further along the broad, moorland ridge.

Barrerneen
Retrace your steps to the corner of the fence which was reached earlier.

Continue walking along the fence to reach a small cairn on the top of a moorland rise. The name Barrerneen has been borrowed from a feature further along the moorland ridge, as the actual summit has no name.

The fence can be used as a line of descent, leading down to an access road serving a remote farmstead. Turn right to walk down the road, then left at a curiously shaped road junction. This last road returns to Drehideighteragh Bridge.

Alternatives:

A fine, high-level challenge walk could start with these mountains, perhaps in reverse order, continuing along the Cork/Kerry boundary all the way along the rugged crest of the Beara peninsula. All the mountains in Walks 26, 27, 28 and 29 would be linked. It's an expedition only for the toughest mountain walkers as there is some rough country between the walks described.

WALK 27:

Summit:	Coomnadiha 2,116ft (645m) V 848600
Character:	A rugged, isolated mountain with a difficult ascent.
Distance:	4 miles (6 kilometres).
Maps:	1:50,000 Sheet 85. Half Inch Sheet 24.
Start/Finish:	Baurearagh.
Getting There:	Baurearagh is the glen served by a minor road near Bunane, which is reached from the main N71 road between Glengarriff and Kenmare.

THE ROUTE

Coomnadiha

Start this walk as far along the Baurearagh road as possible. A track zig-zags up past the last buildings, offering a view of the tremendous cliff-line falling from Caha. The zig-zag track just about expires on a gap on the rugged ridge. Follow this ridge south-westwards, picking a careful route along grassy ledges between rocky outcrops. A tiny lough will be noticed and it's best to pick a way down to it rather than tackle any more of the awkward ridge. Climb uphill from the lough, following a steep, grassy slope into a wide hollow. The slope becomes heathery towards

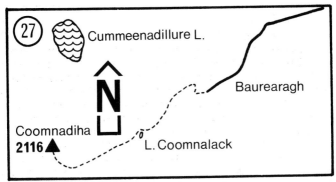

the top. Turn right across an area of peat hags to reach the summit trig point. The nearby summit of Caha, from which the Caha Mountains presumably take their name, doesn't really merit a separate listing. Walk back down to Baurearagh, if you can remember your fiddly route along the rugged ridge below.

Alternatives:

An ascent could be made from Glantrasna, avoiding cliffs. Contours between Coomnadiha and Knockowen suggest fairly easy walking, but the whole distance between the mountains is a wilderness of rocky outcrops, pools and bogs, which can be difficult in mist.

WALK 28:

Summit:	Knockowen	2,169ft (661m) V 808553
Character:	A rocky climb from the Healy Pass to a solitary summit.	
Distance:	5 miles (8 kilometres).	
Maps:	1:50,000 Sheet 84. Half Inch Sheet 24.	
Start/Finish:	The Healy Pass.	
Getting There:	The Healy Pass can be reached from Lauragh or Adrigole - both of which are on the R574 road.	

THE ROUTE

Knockowen (cnoc Eoghain = hill of Owen)

The top of the Healy Pass is exceptionally rocky and the drive over it is quite popular. Anyone who wants to get to grips with this type of terrain will have to pick a route uphill north-eastwards from the pass. If a direct line seems too rocky, then cross to the Glanmore side of the pass and weave up through various outcrops to make an ascent from that side. As height is gained, there are opportunities to take grassier lines. The gradient eases around the half-way mark and a path has been trodden along the ridge. A final pull leads to the summit, which is marked by a cairn sitting on a rib of rock. Knockowen is a good place to sit and study the bleaker parts of the Caha Mountains, but there are also views across to the big mountains of the Iveragh peninsula. Walk back down to the Healy Pass, taking care over the final part of the descent. There is a little hut selling sweets, drinks and souvenirs.

Alternatives:

The country between Knockowen and Coomnadiha is a wilderness of rocky outcrops, pools and bogs, which can be difficult in mist. A more likely alternative seems to be a link with Hungry Hill, but this too is guarded by some awkward expanses of rock, where clear weather would be a definite advantage.

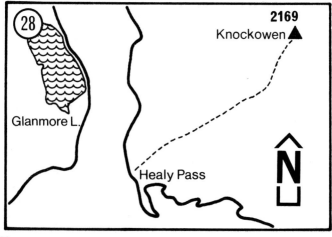

WALK 29:

Summits:	Maulin	2,044ft (623m)	V 713505
	Hungry Hill	2,251ft (686m)	V 761697
Character:	Two rugged mountains connected by a rocky, boggy ridge.		
Distance:	15 miles (24 kilometres).		
Maps:	1:50,000 Sheet 84. Half Inch Sheet 24.		
Start/Finish:	Glanmore Lake Youth Hostel.		
Getting There:	The Youth Hostel can be reached via a minor road from Lauragh, off the R571 road.		

THE ROUTE

Maulin (maolín = little bald hill)

From the Youth Hostel, follow the minor road further into Glanmore. The head of the glen appears to split into two, so take a narrow road on the left to reach the correct head. A waterfall will be seen beyond the last building and a narrow path of sorts can be traced up alongside it. A high valley lies upstream of the waterfall - a remote and boggy place flanked by outcrops of rock. Walk all the way to the head of this valley, where there is a sudden view over to Glenbeg. Turn left at this point and pick a way up a rocky slope. The rocks give way to boggy ground, leading to the broad top of Maulin. The summit is marked by a solitary stone perched on a little bump. Views embrace the rugged mountains and hills of both the Beara and Iveragh peninsulas.

Hungry Hill (cnoc daod = hill of envy)

Hungry Hill lies due east of Maulin, but direct lines simply cannot be followed in this sort of country. Try to stick to the following route to exploit the easiest available course. First, descend north-eastwards from Maulin, taking care on a steep, rocky descent to reach a gap. Look ahead to spot a strip of grass which offers the best way onto the top of Knocknagree. The top of this hill is rocky and boggy, bearing a summit cairn. Descend to Glas Lough - the largest of a group of small loughs roughly south-eastwards from Knocknagree. Now bear right to gain what passes for the main ridge in this contorted country. Surprisingly, blobs of paint have been applied to boulders and outcrops, leaving the ascent of Hungry Hill a simple matter of following waymarks. There is still

93

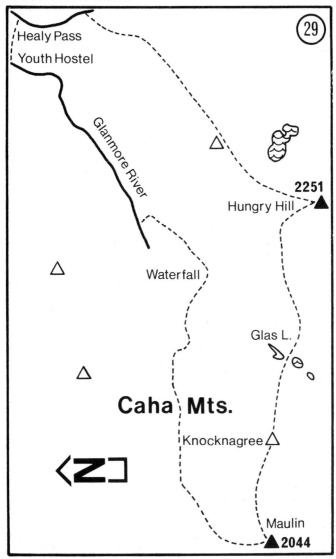

Healy Pass

Youth Hostel

Glanmore River

(29)

2251

Hungry Hill ▲

Waterfall

Glas L.

Caha Mts.

Knocknagree △

Maulin

▲**2044**

the rock and bog to contend with, then the waymarks end a little short of the top of Hungry Hill. A final gentle slope leads to the summit trig point and cairn. There is also a cairn on a nearby shoulder which offers good views over Bantry Bay.

Descend northwards, but start turning north-eastwards after only a short way. Take care on this line of descent as easy grassy terraces and ridges of rock tend to pull walkers towards a ferocious cliff face. Scramble over the rock ridges one after the other to descend to a gap. To play safe - aim rather more towards Glanmore, then later correct yourself to reach the gap. Keep roughly to the main ridge heading north-east towards the Healy Pass. Outflank any minor summits and rocky outcrops and stick to the easiest course. It's also a good idea to descend to the road a little before the top of the Healy Pass, avoiding massive blocks of rock. Walk past the little hut which sells sweets, drinks and souvenirs, then pass the statues of the Crucifixion scene on the top of the pass. The road runs downhill, then a small sign points out a direct line down a steep slope to return to Glanmore Lake Youth Hostel.

Alternatives:
Both Maulin and Hungry Hill can be reached by gentler routes on their southern slopes, but the route offered above caters for youth hostellers based in Glanmore. The two mountains could be covered as described, then tough walkers could continue over Knockowen and Coomnadiha to reach distant Knockboy and its satellite summits. This walk stays on the bleak, boggy, rocky crest of the Caha Mountains and is one of the toughest ridge walks on offer. Details of sections are contained in Walks 26, 27, 28 & 29.

WALK 30:

Summit:	Crohane 2,162ft (659m) W 050829
Character:	A fine, solitary peak climbed via a good track.
Distance:	5 miles (8 kilometres).
Maps:	1:50,000 Sheet 79. Half Inch Sheet 21.
Start/Finish:	East of Lough Guitane.
Getting There:	Lough Guitane can be reached from Muckross, on the main N71 road, or Glenflesk, on the main N22 road. Both roads run from Killarney.

THE ROUTE

Crohane (cruachán = steep-sided mountain)

Start this walk between Lough Guitane and Glenflesk, on the highest part of the minor road connecting the two places. A narrow road runs opposite a two-storey house, heading southwards to pass some bungalows before reaching a farm. Keep to the right of the farm, following an enclosed track until it overlooks Lough Guitane. Turn left and go through gates to reach the open, heathery slopes of the mountain. A prominent track has been cut in a series of zig-zags on these steep slopes, easing the gradient on the ascent. The track doesn't quite reach the top of Crohane, but there is only a short climb from its end. Walk along the high shoulder of the mountain to reach a narrow crest ending at the summit cairn. Good views take in the mountains of Kerry and West Cork. Walk back down the track for the descent.

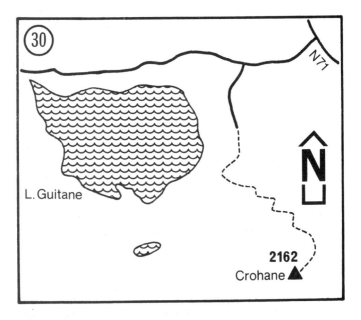

Alternatives:

Most of Crohane's lower slopes are exceptionally rugged. An ascent from Loo Bridge is possible, but the terrain is very hard. It's possible to head towards Mangerton, but be sure to keep well to the south of Bennaunmore, as this rocky hump is pretty awkward.

WALK 31:

Summits:	Mangerton North Top	2,570ft (782m)	V	984818
	Mangerton Mountain	2,756ft (839m)	V	980808
	Stoompa	2,281ft (694m)	W	007820
Character:	A fairly straightforward circuit of three mountain summits, but ending with a difficult moorland trudge to return to the starting point.			
Distance:	10 miles (16 kilometres).			
Maps:	1:50,000 Sheets 78 & 79. Half Inch Sheets 20 or 21.			
	1:25,000 Sheet - Killarney National Park.			
Start/Finish:	Tooreencormick.			
Getting There:	From Muckross, on the main N71 road, follow signposts for Mangerton Mountain to reach a viewpoint car park.			

THE ROUTE

Mangerton North Top

There is a viewpoint car park on the minor road at Tooreencormick, overlooking the Lakes of Killarney. Walk further along the road, looking out for a left turn towards the end. A track crosses a concrete bridge and runs gently uphill. Go through a gate in a fence to reach the open mountainside. Trace an old track which runs uphill alongside a stream. The track later crosses the stream by way of a ford. Keep going uphill, noting that the track is sometimes stony, boggy or overgrown. Despite this, it offers the best means of progress across featureless slopes. The way becomes better surfaced as it swings across heathery slopes and reaches an old gateway in a ruined boundary wall. Walk alongside the wall, following a boggy path uphill. The wall runs into a small lough in the Devil's Punch Bowl. Don't go down to the shore of the lough, but turn left

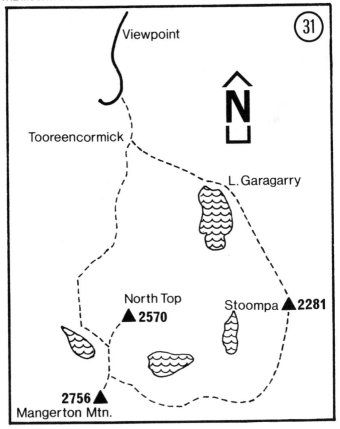

beforehand to follow a bouldery, heathery ridge to a gap. Another left turn on the gap leads to the final part of the ascent to the North Top. Simple grass and heather slopes give way to a broad summit of moss and heather. There is only a small cairn to mark the summit.

Mangerton Mountain (móin phortach = long grassed bog)
Return to the gap below the North Top, which overlooks the loughs in both the Devil's Punch Bowl and Glennacappul. Head straight up a steep, but safe ridge between these two great coums. The ridge

suddenly ends on the edge of Mangerton's broad plateau. In mist, the summit could be difficult to locate, though there is a sparse line of marker stones to lead you there if you are roughly on course. A broad expanse of long, wet grass is broken only by the summit trig point. The plateau rather spoils otherwise extensive views, but ranges of mountains throughout Kerry and West Cork can be identified.

Stoompa (stumpa = stump)

Return to the rocky edge of the Mangerton plateau and turn right. It's a simple matter to follow the edge overlooking Glennacappul, enjoying fine views of its three loughs while keeping clear of higher, boggier areas. After crossing a rugged little gap, a path leads to the top of Stoompa. The summit is bouldery and heathery, marked with a cairn. A minor summit to the east isn't really worth bothering about and I haven't given it a separate listing. It's a vague, unmarked rise overshadowed by Stoompa.

Descend towards the outflow of Lough Garragarry, taking care on the steep, heathery, stony slopes of Stoompa. A north-westwards line across a rugged moorland eventually links with the track used on the outward journey, returning to the road at Tooreencormick.

Alternatives:

A reasonably easy line is available south-west from Mangerton Mountain to link with Walk 32 on Dromderalough. A much tougher walk leads from Stoompa towards Crohane. If tempted to use this latter option, then keep well south of Bennaunmore, as this rocky hump is pretty awkward.

WALK 32:

Summits:	Knockbrack	2,005ft (610m)	V 954779
	Dromderalough	2,139ft (650m)	V 960789
Character:	Two outlying summits, properly part of Mangerton Mountain, which are rugged but fairly easy to cover.		
Distance:	4 miles (6 kilometres).		
Maps:	1:50,000 Sheet 78. Half Inch Sheet 20 or 21.		
	1:25,000 Sheet - Killarney National Park.		
Start/Finish:	Baurearagh Forest.		
Getting There:	Baurearagh Forest is at the end of a minor road off the R569 road between Kenmare and Kilgarvan.		

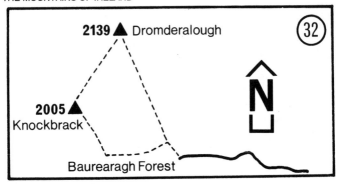

THE ROUTE

Knockbrack (cnoc an bhráca = speckled hill)
On reaching the entrance to Baurearagh Forest, simply follow the forest fence uphill. It runs north-west, then west, then north-west again. The first part crosses tussocky moorlands, while the final part becomes ever steeper and rockier. Once on top of Knockbrack, there are at least three humps which could claim to be the summit, with other lesser eminences scattered all around.

Dromderalough (druim doire loch = hill of the oakwood lake)
Follow a broad, rocky crest roughly north-eastwards, crossing a rocky gap before scrambling up the slopes of Dromderalough. There is, surprisingly, a vague path and a sparse line of cairns to follow. The summit cairn stands on a rocky outcrop. Views across the Iveragh peninsula are quite good.

A descent can be made south-eastwards, taking care on a steep, rocky slope at first. Tussocky grass moorlands need to be crossed to return to the entrance of Baurearagh Forest.

Alternatives:

Ascents based on the Kerry Way, to the north, aren't particularly recommended as the intervening country is rather rough and boggy. However, a continuation from Dromderalough to the summit of Mangerton Mountain is really quite easy. In the other direction, it's rather a long, hard walk to link with Walk 33, but this could be the start of a great expedition, staying on the high mountains all the way through the

Looking towards Mangerton Mountain from Dromderalough

Iveragh peninsula. The suggestion is made for the hardiest of mountain walkers to consider - it's not a trip to be undertaken lightly.

WALK 33:

Summits:	Boughil	2,065ft (631m)	V 842765
	Knocknacappul	2,091ft (639m)	V 834767
	Knocklomena	2,097ft (641m)	V 797766
Character:	Three rocky mountains linked by a hard, but fairly straightforward ridge, ending with a long road-walk.		
Distance:	10 miles (16 kilometres).		
Maps:	1:50,000 Sheet 78. Half Inch Sheets 20 or 21.		
	1:25,000 Sheet - Macgillycuddy's Reeks.		
Start/Finish:	Lough Barfinnihy.		
Getting There:	Lough Barfinnihy is just west of Moll's Gap, so it can be approached via the main N71 road, between Killarney and Kenmare, the R568 road from Sneem, or a minor road from the Black Valley.		

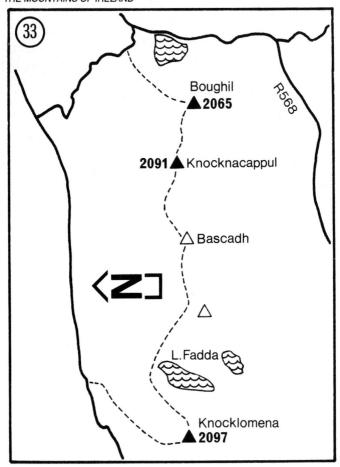

THE ROUTE

Boughil (buachaill = cowherd)

Start the walk by following the Black Valley road away from Lough Barfinnihy - certainly no further than a small culvert. Climb steeply uphill, picking any decent-looking route along grassy lines between outcrops of rock. Some parts of the ascent can be wet. A final steep pull leads to

102

Knocklomena rising above Lough Fadda

a fairly level top. A fence crosses the summit and there is a small cairn.

Knocknacappul (cnoc na gcappul = hill of the horse)
Follow the fence from the summit of Boughil down to a narrow gap. The way down is steep and rugged. For the ascent of Knocknacappul, follow a grassy strip between rock outcrops. A metal post marks the summit of the mountain.

Knocklomena (cnoc an mheannáin = hill of the pinnacle)
Follow the main ridge further westwards, descending to cross another narrow gap. Climb steeply onto a hill called Bascadh and follow a fence all the way along its crest. On reaching a shallow gap, bear right and descend via increasingly rugged slopes to reach the head of Lough Fadda. Look for an easy way though a band of rock on the next ascent, then simply walk up a grassy slope passing outcrops of rock. Knocklomena has a broad top with a metal post and a small cairn on the summit.

Any line roughly northwards can be used for the descent, picking up the line of a fence which can be followed down a shoulder of the mountain to reach a road on a gap. Turn right and follow the road down into the glen, later turning right to take a twisting road back up to Lough Barfinnihy.

Alternatives:
Instead of completing this circuit with a road-walk, it's a fairly easy matter
to climb from the road on the gap to reach the summit of Stumpa Duloigh.
If pursuing this course and aiming to complete Walk 34, then be sure to
allow plenty of time. It's very useful if you can arrange to be collected by
someone once you reach the head of the Black Valley.

WALK 34:

Summits:	Broaghnabinnia	2,440ft (745m)	V 802814
	Stumpa Duloigh	2,572ft (784m)	V 787794
	Stumpa West Top	2,175ft (663m)	V 778789

Character:	A fine, rugged circuit of three mountains, which can be difficult at the start and finish of the walk.
Distance:	10 miles (16 kilometres).
Maps:	1:50,000 Sheet 78. Half Inch Sheets 20 or 21.
	1:25,000 Sheet - Macgillycuddy's Reeks.
Start/Finish:	The Roisin Lake.
Getting There:	The Roisin Lake is at the head of the Black Valley, reached before the road zig-zags steeply uphill.

THE ROUTE

Broaghnabinnia (bruach na binne = edge of the mountain)
Follow a short track past the Roisin Lake (also known as Lough Reagh),
then follow a river steeply upstream. It's maybe a better idea to ascend
the steep, rugged nose between this river and the main river. The slopes
of Broaghnabinnia are steep, but from this side there is very little rock.
It's a long slog up these slopes, but eventually the gradient eases to
reveal a broad top. A fence crosses the summit and there are good
close-up views of the Reeks ridge. Bird's-eye views of the glens are
available from the edge of Broaghnabinnia.

Stumpa Duloigh (stumpa dubh loch = stump of the black lake)
Retrace steps down the flanks of Broaghnabinnia, perhaps using a
sheep-path to traverse to a rocky gap on the way to Stumpa Duloigh. A
direct line from the summit of Broaghnabinnia to reach this gap is not

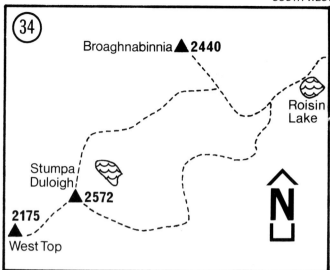

recommended as there is too much outcropping rock and a danger of walkers getting into difficulties. Slow progress is almost guaranteed while negotiating the gap, but as height is gained there are fewer difficulties. A steep ridge leads up onto Stumpa Duloigh. There are all sorts of minor summits along this ridge, which could be confusing in mist. In clear weather there will be no mistaking the highest summit.

Stumpa West Top

Head south-westwards from Stumpa Duloigh - a line which has a fence as a guide across a low gap, leading up to a subsidiary summit. This is a hummocky place, ending with an outcrop of rock marking the summit.

We're a long way from the Roisin Lake and the "descent" actually starts with the re-ascent of Stumpa Duloigh. Once back on the main ridge, turn right and follow it downhill. The ridge falls gently at first, then suddenly steepens to drop to a gap where a fence is encountered. A left turn leads down a very steep and rugged slope to reach the headwaters of the Gearhameen River. Take care over this descent, looking ahead to gauge the best course. Even following the river downstream can be hard work and there are some boggy patches. It's best to avoid a waterfall on the lower reaches of the river by charting a course down a rugged nose to the left. Once at the foot of this nose, exit via the short track near the Roisin Lake.

Alternatives:
Instead of completing a circuit by returning to the Black Valley, the walk can be ended by crossing rugged little hills between Stumpa West Top and the Ballaghbeama Gap. If you can arrange to be picked up on the gap it makes the walk so much easier. It's also possible to cross the gap and link this walk with Walk 35. A link with Walk 33 is also an idea worth considering.

WALK 35:

Summits:	Mullaghanattin	2,539ft (773m)	V 739773
	Beann North Top	2,273ft (692m)	V 731771
	Beann	2,470ft (752m)	V 726764
	Beann West Top	2,155ft (657m)	V 719760
	Beann South Top	2,100ft (639m)	V 728756

Character:	A circuit around five mountain summits arranged around The Pocket, featuring some steep slopes.
Distance:	8 miles (13 kilometres).
Maps:	1:50,000 Sheet 78. Half Inch Sheet 20.
	1:25,000 Sheet - Macgillycuddy's Reeks.
Start/Finish:	Tooreenahone.
Getting There:	Tooreenahone is at the end of a minor road on the north side of the R568 road between Sneem and Moll's Gap.

THE ROUTE

Mullaghanattin (mullach an aitinn = summit of the furze)
From the end of the tarmac road at Tooreenahone, walk along a track to reach the last buildings in the glen, then cross a river. Follow the river to its source on the eastern side of Mullaghanattin. This is a steep, often wet climb, but mostly on grass. Once the high gap has been reached, turn left to follow a fence along the steep shoulder of the mountain. The fence doesn't go to the top, so keep to the steepest ground ahead to

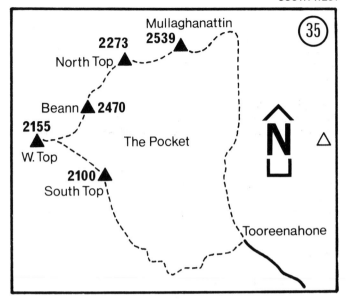

reach the summit. There is a trig point and fine views over the mountains of the Iveragh peninsula.

Beann North Top
A steep, grassy descent roughly south-westwards from the summit of Mullaghanattin rejoins the fence, which offers a safe guide down to a narrow, rocky gap. The fence leads across the flank of the North Top, so climb steeply up broken rocky ground from the gap. There is a memorial to a walker who was killed here, so take care. After this initial stiff pull, the gradient eases, but this subsidiary summit is rocky all the way to the top.

Beann (binn = mountain)
The North Top is quite overshadowed by both Mullaghanattin and Beann. Head towards Beann, following the fence up its slopes. From the summit, there is a good view back to Mullaghanattin.

107

Beann West Top

Follow the broad crest of Beann for a short way, then head off to the right and follow a rugged spur down to a narrow gap. A short climb leads up to another subsidiary summit of Beann. There are other humps and bumps along the same ridge, but they don't qualify as separate summits.

Beann South Top

Walk back down to the narrow gap. There's no need to climb back onto Beann, but simply follow a sheep-path across its slopes from one gap to another. The direction is south-eastwards, then a quick ascent leads to the final subsidiary of Beann.

Descend south-eastwards from the summit - the aim being to join a track which leads down to a huddle of farm buildings. Care needs to be taken on this course in mist, as there is a danger of being drawn onto steep, rugged ground, or missing the track entirely. From the farm, follow the access road across the River Blackwater, returning to Tooreenahone.

Alternatives:

This is a neat and impressive walk in its own right, though there is some awkward dodging about for subsidiary summits. An ascent could be made from the Ballaghbeama Gap - a tough way of gaining the summit of Mullaghanattin. A fine, rugged ridge-walk can also be enjoyed by walking from Beann towards Finnararagh, linking with Walk 36. Like most walks in these mountains, it's not an option for a misty day as walkers could be drawn off course and get into difficulties.

WALK 36:

Summits:	Knocknagantee	2,220ft (676m)	V 668730
	Knockmoyle	2,245ft (684m)	V 665750
	Coomura	2,185ft (666m)	V 677752
	Coomanassig	2,086ft (636m)	V 680734
	Finnararagh	2,185ft (667m)	V 697737
Character:	Five mountains with rocky faces, which can be linked one to another by fairly easy routes. The end of the walk, however, crosses some difficult terrain.		
Distance:	12 miles (19 kilometres).		
Maps:	1:50,000 Sheets 78 or 83. Half Inch Sheet 20.		

Start/Finish: On a road near the head of Sneem River.

Getting There: Sneem is on the main N70 road. Follow a minor road
                    north-west of town to trace the Sneem River.

THE ROUTE

Knocknagantee (cnoc na gcainnte = hill of conversation)
The starting point for the walk is a lonely fork in the road alongside the
Sneem River. Follow the road to the left, heading for the last farm. Turn
right immediately on reaching the farm and walk along a broad track.
This track can be seen to cut great zig-zags across the face of
Knocknagantee. Although rough and stony in places, the track offers the
best means of climbing the mountain. It ends on reaching the grassy
shoulder of Knocknagantee, but a simple walk further uphill quickly
leads to the summit. A fence is crossed by a stile to reach the summit
cairn. Views all round reveal that the other mountains in this group rise
from a broad depression, so there are no great ascents to wrestle with
while walking round them.

Knockmoyle (cnoc maol = bald hill)
Follow the fence gently downhill from Knocknagantee, crossing a broad,
rocky and boggy gap. The fence then runs uphill, but as it doesn't
actually reach the summit of Knockmoyle, you'll have to branch off to the
right and make your own way there. Walk straight uphill on boggy
ground. There is another fence crossing the summit, but nothing marks
the highest part of the mountain.

Coomura (cúm fhuar = cold hollow)
The deep coum between Knockmoyle and the next mountain is called
Coomura. I'm borrowing this name to tag onto the mountain, which is
otherwise nameless. Follow the fence down from Knockmoyle, heading
south-eastwards to reach the gap between the mountains. This is a
boggy, bouldery area just off the line of the fence. Walk straight up a
boggy slope, where there are no aids to navigation, to reach the top of
the mountain. There is nothing to mark the summit.

Coomanassig
Again, the name of a deep coum is being used to label an unnamed
summit. Descend from Coomura to rejoin the fence on the boggy,

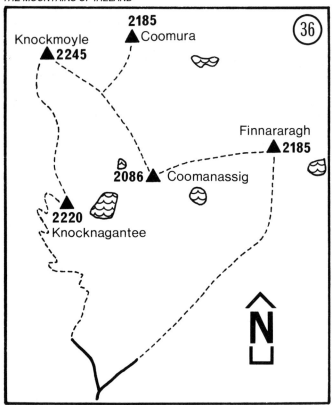

bouldery gap. Next, turn left to follow the fence down to a lower, boggy, bouldery gap. The fence doesn't quite reach the gap, so you'll have to pick your own way across it. On the ascent from the gap, steer a course between areas of rock and bog. There is a small cairn on the summit of the mountain. The walk so far has described a sort of square shape so we can look back at the rugged face of Knocknagantee, rising above Eagles Lough.

Finnararagh (fionn bhogach = fair soft bog)
Head roughly westwards to cross yet another rocky, boggy gap, then

follow a broad, rugged crest to reach the top of Finnararagh. There is a small cairn marking the summit.

Descend carefully southwards, picking a line down a rugged slope. On reaching a prominent stream, alter direction and head south-west. Aim for a group of farm buildings, tackling small streams and fences as they arise. Follow the access road away from the farm to return to the lonely fork in the road near the Sneem River. The descent from Finnararagh is probably the hardest part of the day's walk.

Alternatives:
The walk as described is probably the best way to cover these five mountains, though they could also be attempted as a circuit from Lissatinnig. Consider also the rugged ridge-walk from Finnararagh to link with Walk 35 at Beann. There's also an awkward, complex ridge-walk in the other direction linking Knocknagantee with Coomcallee and Walk 37. It's while walking over these mountains that we can appreciate how exposed and contorted the underlying rock is, making the mountains of Kerry the roughest in Ireland.

WALK 37:

Summits:	Coomcallee	2,135ft (650m)	V 625676
	Coomcallee West Top	2,218ft (676m)	V 593683
Character:	A fairly easy walk over the two summits of Coomcallee.		
Distance:	10 miles (16 kilometres).		
Maps:	1:50,000 Sheets 83 or 84. Half Inch Sheets 20 & 24.		
Start/Finish:	Glenmore School.		
Getting There:	Glenmore School, or the Teach Bríde Museum, can be reached by following a minor road into Glenmore from the main N70 road at Waterville.		

THE ROUTE
Coomcallee (cúm na cailleach = hollow of the old woman)
Follow the minor road from Glenmore School, now the Teach Bríde Museum, towards the head of Glenmore. After passing the last buildings,

111

**Looking from Waterville towards Coomcallee,
far beyond Lough Currane**

a broad track continues further. This begins to climb uphill in a series of zig-zags and ends just before reaching a gap between the two summits of the mountain. You could head either left or right from the gap, depending on which summit you want to visit first. For the sake of argument, we'll turn right, walking up a short slope before crossing a minor hump. A broad gap lies beyond and once across this a final ascent leads to a boggy summit crowned with peat hags.

Coomcallee West Top
Walk back to the lowest gap, then climb another slope, crossing another minor hump and broad gap to reach the other summit of Coomcallee. This route allows a peep into a deep, rocky coum, then follows a groove across mossy ground to reach the summit trig point. Walk back to the lowest gap to follow the zig-zag track back down into Glenmore.

Alternatives:
A more difficult ascent is available from the northern slopes of Coomcallee. I also feel like issuing a challenge to the toughest mountain walkers in Ireland. This is a long, hard expedition, starting with the ascent of Coomcallee. I'm suggesting that a rugged, high-level trek could be

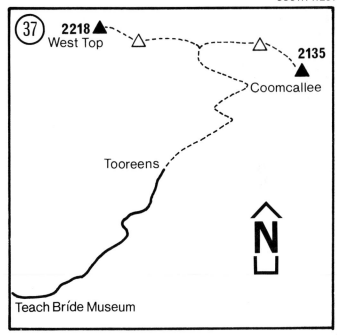

enjoyed over all the mountain summits from Walks 37, 36, 35, 34, 33, 32, 31, & 30. Why end on Crohane? You could continue towards The Paps and away into West Cork. Facilities on this mountain traverse are extremely limited - the only point of refreshment being at Moll's Gap. This is perhaps the longest, hardest, high-level route which could be attempted in Ireland. Check it out on a map - even if the idea doesn't appeal to you.

WALK 38:

Summits:	Knocknadobar	2,267ft (691m)	V	507845
	Knocknadobar East Top	2,087ft (636m)	V	529858
	Knocknadobar Far East Top	2,000ft (610m)	V	537860

Character:	A tough ascent via the Stations of the Cross, followed by a fairly easy walk over the three summits of Knocknadobar.
Distance:	12 miles (19 kilometres).
Maps:	1:50,000 Sheet 83. Half Inch Sheet 20.
Start/Finish:	On the road to Coonanna Harbour.
Getting There:	Coonanna Harbour can be reached from Cahirsiveen or Doonane, both of which are on the main N70 road.

THE ROUTE

Knocknadobar (cnoc na dtobar = hill of the wells)

The road to Coonanna Harbour passes a small wayside grotto, then the walk starts on the right-hand side of the road, at the second gate. Cross a wet field and go through a small gate to reach a concrete cross. This is set with a scene from the Passion of Christ and inscribed with a Roman numeral I. (Walkers unfamiliar with the Stations of the Cross need only note that there are fourteen in the series, all similar to this first one.) At first the slopes are rocky and covered in bracken. Later they steepen and

The Stations of the Cross lead to the summit of Knocknadobar

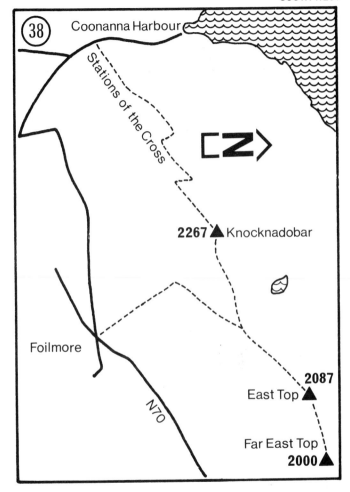

become heathery. In places the path is vague, so marker posts show the way from one Station to another. The final part of the ascent follows a narrow ridge to the 14th Station. Beyond is a much larger cross - the Canon's Cross. The summit trig point stands a little further away, on a broad, stony area.

Knocknadobar East Top

Walk eastwards, then north-eastwards to pick up a vague path along the edge of a deep coum. There is a boggy, grassy gap to cross, then a line of upended stones points the way uphill. These don't go far, but could be a useful navigational aid in mist. By walking uphill in the direction they indicate, the top of the subsidiary will be reached. Heather slopes give way to a broad area of stones bound by moss. The summit is marked with a cairn.

Knocknadobar Far East Top

A short walk further along the broad crest of the mountain crosses a gap and leads up to another stony area. Again, the summit of this subsidiary is marked with a cairn.

Descents can be made southwards to the Ring of Kerry road, but this leaves a long road-walk back to the start. It's better to walk back over the East Top, descend to the lowest gap, then bear left to pick up a vague path which crosses the lower slopes of Knocknadobar. This was once a prominent track, but is now quite difficult to trace. You'll notice another track which heads straight down to the road. Follow this, turning right along the road to return to the start along the Coonanna Harbour road.

WALK 39:

Summits:	Meenteog	2,350ft (715m)	V 638827
	Coomacarrea	2,541ft (772m)	V 611826
	Teermoyle Mountain	2,442ft (760m)	V 604833
	Mullaghnarakill	2,182ft (665m)	V 601850
	Been Hill	2,130ft (650m)	V 589854
	Beenmore	2,199ft (669m)	V 596868
	Drung Hill	2,104ft (640m)	V 603878
Character:	Seven mountain summits linked by a fairly straightforward ridge-walk, but starting with a steep, rocky ascent.		
Distance:	12 miles (20 kilometres).		
Maps:	1:50,000 Sheets 78 & 83. Half Inch Sheet 20.		
Start/Finish:	Coomsaharn Lake.		
Getting There:	Coomsaharn can be reached via a minor road from Glenbeigh, which is itself on the main N70 road.		

THE ROUTE

Meenteog (muing = flat, boggy, grassy place)
Don't follow the tarmac road to its very end at Coomsaharn Lake, but walk along a track on the left to reach a small group of buildings at the foot of Knocknaman. Follow a fence uphill from a gate, then cross the fence and continue up the steep and rugged face of the mountain, looking for any evidence of a trodden path. Above all the rocky outcrops is a broad, moorland crest. Follow this uphill and keep to the edge of Coomeeneragh. There is a fence around the edge of the coum and this reaches the summit of Meenteog, which is marked with a small cairn.

Coomacarrea (cúm na chaorach = hollow of the sheep)
A broad moorland slope descends gradually to the west of Meenteog. There is a fence nearby, but don't follow it as it leads away from the main ridge. Instead, look out for an old boundary wall and ditch which can be traced along the broad crest to a wide gap. Excellent views take in Coomsaharn and its rocky headwall. The wall and ditch are plain to follow uphill, but it's a boggy ditch and a line of fenceposts which finally cross the top of the mountain. The summit is broad, grassy and unmarked.

Teermoyle Mountain (tír maol = bald land)
The remains of the boundary ditch are followed on the descent from Coomacarrea but the accompanying fenceposts disappear. There is a fence on the next broad gap, then the ditch becomes rather vague on the gentle slopes climbing towards the top of Teermoyle Mountain. The vague line of the ditch stays near the edge of Coomsaharn, so a short detour to the left is needed to reach the top of Teermoyle Mountain. Cross soft ground, continuing over moss and stones to reach a summit lump of peat.

Mullaghnarakill
On the descent from Teermoyle Mountain, locate the boundary ditch and mound which lead down broad slopes of peat and stones. A fence later leads down to a broad gap overlooking Coomaglaslaw. The fence suddenly turns left, so keep walking uphill, tracing the stony mound to the summit of Mullaghnarakill. Large slabs of rock lie on this point.

Been Hill (binn = mountain)
If you keep to the moorland crest between Mullaghnarakill and Been Hill,

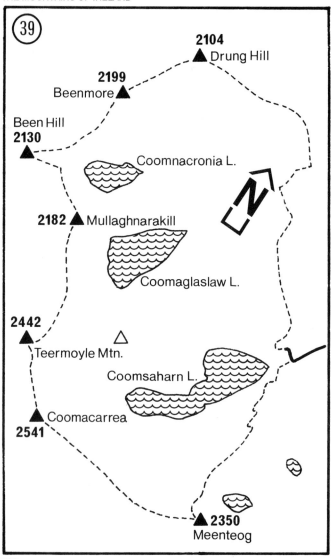

39

2104
▲ Drung Hill

2199
Beenmore ▲

Been Hill
2130
▲

Coomnacronia L.

N

2182 ▲ Mullaghnarakill

Coomaglaslaw L.

2442
▲
Teermoyle Mtn.
△

Coomsaharn L.

▲ Coomacarrea
2541

▲ **2350**
Meenteog

you'll be following an unmarked route through an area of peat hags. It's better to continue along the boundary ditch, which stays on the eastern side of Been Hill. The ditch should be followed across a couple of small streams, then walkers should turn left to trace a line of old fenceposts uphill. The grassy summit of Been Hill is crossed by another fence, but is otherwise unmarked.

Beenmore (binn mhór = big mountain)
Turn right to follow the fence down from Been Hill. It doesn't go all the way down to a peaty, rocky gap, which is actually crossed by the now familiar form of the old boundary ditch. The ascent of Beenmore from the gap is heathery. Simply follow a stony mound uphill, passing a small stone shelter before reaching the top. There is a summit cairn.

Drung Hill
A narrow, heathery ridge with a path along it leads north-east from Beenmore to Drung Hill. An easy ascent leads to a summit trig point and cairn. Throughout the whole of this walk, excellent views have ranged across the mountains of the Iveragh peninsula. On the final part of the walk, the mountains of the Dingle peninsula are also prominent.

Descend steeply eastwards down heathery slopes which become gentler as a long ridge is reached. The idea is to pick a line down to a bog road, which can be seen leading back to Coomsaharn.

Alternatives:
Great zig-zag tracks lead up the western sides of these mountains, but approaches from that side do not lend themselves to a circular route. At the end of this walk, you could descend to Mountain Stage, which is a handy place for someone to meet you. It's also possible to extend the walk by including an ascent of Colly, which is detailed on Walk 40.

WALK 40:

Summit:	Colly	2,238ft (679m) V 651808
Character:	A fairly simple ascent of a fine, solitary peak.	
Distance:	3 miles (5 kilometres).	
Maps:	1:50,000 Sheet 78. Half Inch Sheet 20.	
Start/Finish:	Coomaspeara.	

Getting There: Coomaspeara is at the end of a minor road which could be reached from Waterville, Cahirsiveen or Glencar, after negotiating many other minor roads.

THE ROUTE

Colly (coill = wood)
A huddle of colourful farm buildings stand at the head of Coomaspeara. A track zig-zags uphill, ending near a gap. There is a wall and fence which can be followed uphill from the gap, but when these suddenly turn left you must turn right. A path leads uphill and finally follows a narrow ridge of rock and heather. The summit of Colly is marked by a cairn and a metal post. There are good views around the mountains of the Iveragh peninsula, as Colly occupies a fairly central position in relation to them.

Alternatives:
You could link the ascent of Colly with all the mountains covered on Walk 39. The connecting ridge is hummocky, but fairly easy to walk along, then an ascent leads onto Meenteog.

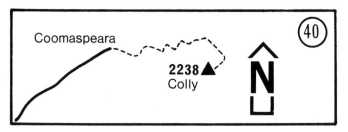

WALK 41:

Summits:				
Skregmore West Top	2,450ft	(747m)	V	785860
Skregmore	2,790ft	(848m)	V	792860
Skregmore East Top	2,792ft	(851m)	V	796858
Knockbrinnea	2,782ft	(854m)	V	808858
Beenkeragh	3,314ft	(1,010m)	V	801853
Carrauntoohil	3,414ft	(1,039m)	V	803844
Caher	3,284ft	(1,001m)	V	792839
Caher West Top	3,200ft	(975m)	V	790840

Character:	A splendid, but difficult circuit of Ireland's highest mountains. Some scrambling is called for between the summits of Beenkeragh and Carrauntoohil, following an exposed rocky ridge. Altogether, eight summits are covered.
Distance:	9½ miles (15 kilometres).
Maps:	1:50,000 Sheet 78. Half Inch Sheets 20 or 21.
	1:25,000 Sheet - Macgillycuddy's Reeks.
Start/Finish:	Breanlee.
Getting There:	Breenlee is on a minor road between Killorglin and Glencar, a little north-east of Lough Acoose.

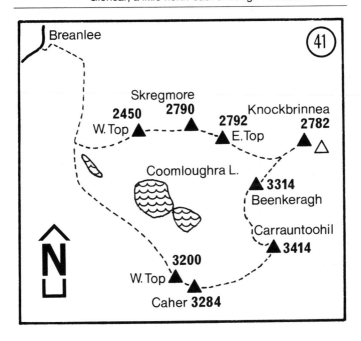

Breanlee

41

Skregmore
2450   **2790**   **2792**   Knockbrinnea
W. Top ▲   ▲   ▲   **2782**
E. Top   ▲ △

Coomloughra L.

▲ **3314**
Beenkeragh

Carrauntoohil
▲ **3414**

3200
W. Top ▲   ▲
Caher **3284**

N

THE ROUTE

Skregmore West Top

A prominent track runs uphill from double gates at the roadside at Breanlee. This is rough and stony at first, but it gets better as it swings southwards across the mountainside to reach a small dam at Lough Eighter. At this point, there is no alternative other than a steep, heathery slog uphill. The way becomes stonier as height is gained, with rocky slabs and outcrops towards the top. There is a cairn on the summit.

Skregmore (screig mhór = big rocky place)

A short, bouldery slope leads down to a grassy gap, then a longer bouldery slope is followed uphill to reach the summit cairn of Skregmore.

Skregmore East Top

A stony slope leads a short way downhill to a grassy gap, then a short, stony slope leads up to another summit cairn.

Knockbrinnea

Leave the three Skregmore summits to descend to a grassy gap bearing a short stretch of wall. Head eastwards across the bouldery face of

The summit cross crowning Ireland's highest point - Carrauntoohil

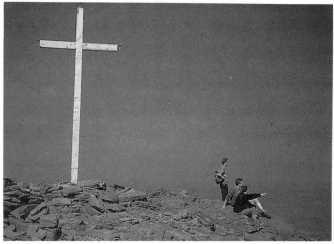

The western summit of Caher, ending the Coomloughra circuit

Beenkeragh, keeping low to exploit a strip of grass running from one gap to another. Once on the far gap, a simple, gradual, bouldery ascent leads onto the summit of Knockbrinnea. There's another summit a little further eastwards, but it doesn't really warrant a separate listing. You could visit it for a good view into the rocky confines of the Hag's Glen, but we've already drifted off the course of the classic horseshoe to reach Knockbrinnea. The "big stuff" is yet to come.

Beenkeragh (binn chaorach = mountain of the sheep)
Beenkeragh is a huge pile of boulders and rocky outcrops. With care, pick out easier lines from the rugged, rocky slopes. Beware of tottery boulders, which could crash out of control if dislodged. Eventually, a short walk along a narrow ridge leads to the summit cairn, offering a fine view ahead to Carrauntoohil.

Carrauntoohil (corrán tuathail = inverted reaping hook)
Carefully descend a steep ridge of rock, aiming for a prominent rocky knob on a lower part of the ridge. You'll be pleased to hear that you don't have to climb over this knob, which would be very difficult. The way forward can be quite exposed at times, but there is generally a choice of lines to by-pass difficulties. It's your choice - the way is hard, but you

123

can make it harder by including interesting moves. A fine, jagged peak rises part way along the ridge and if it were anywhere else I'd treat it as a separate mountain summit. You'll need to get your hands to grips with the rock to cross it. After negotiating this obstacle a steep and bouldery climb leads to the top of Carrauntoohil. The summit furniture includes a trig point, cairn shelter and a huge, metal cross which is a landmark for miles around. Views on a clear day embrace most of the mountains in the south-west of Ireland. We can pile accolade upon accolade and note that Carrauntoohil is the highest mountain in Co Kerry, the Province of Munster, and indeed in all of Ireland. It's a place to linger for a while, weather permitting.

Caher (cathair = fort)

A stony path leads down an easy slope towards Caher, but in mist take care not to be drawn down the path towards the Devil's Ladder. There is a narrow, rocky ridge to cross, but the path keeps just below the serrated crest. The ascent of Caher from the ridge is steep, but without real difficulties. The summit is marked with a cairn.

Caher West Top

Walk a short way downhill to reach a grassy, stony gap. There is an old fence strung across. An ascent up a bouldery slope leads to a summit cairn. There is another cairn further along.

The descent is initially bouldery, then a vague, trodden path can be traced along the broad crest overlooking Coumloughra. Keep to this crest until a short descent leads down to the little dam at Lough Eighter. Follow the stony access track from the dam back down to Breanlee.

Alternatives:

Carrauntoohil is often climbed simply for its own sake. Some people reaching the summit, or attempting to do so, may never climb another mountain in their lives! The usual route is via the Devil's Ladder, which is noted in Walk 42. Experienced mountain walkers may decide to combine Walks 41 and 42, tackling a long, hard day in the mountains. If you can spare the time and energy for this, then you can reap sixteen summits! The circuit around Coumloughra is, however, the best way to gather the summits listed for this walk. It's possible to make an ascent from the Black Valley or Bridia Valley, but these approaches don't lend themselves to a circular walk.

WALK 42:

Summits:	Cnoc na dTarbh	2,150ft (655m)	V 862850
	Cnoc an Bhráca	2,398ft (731m)	V 858854
	Cruach Mhór	3,062ft (932m)	V 841848
	The Big Gun	3,080ft (939m)	V 841845
	Cnoc na Péiste	3,240ft (988m)	V 836842
	Maolán Buí	3,190ft (973m)	V 832838
	Cnoc an Chuillin	3,141ft (958m)	V 823833
	Cnoc na Toinne	2,776ft (845m)	V 811834

Character: A superb ridge walk, covering eight summits. One section is quite difficult, involving scrambling along a rocky ridge. In wet weather the rock can be rather slippery.

Distance: 20 miles (32 kilometres).

Maps: 1:50,000 Sheet 78. Half Inch Sheets 20 or 21.

1:25,000 Sheet - Macgillycuddy's Reeks.

Start/Finish: Kate Kearney's Cotttage.

Getting There: Kate Kearney's Cottage is on the way to the Gap of Dunloe and is best reached from Killarney or Killorglin via Fossa or Beaufort.

THE ROUTE

Cnoc na dTarbh (cnoc na dtarbh = hill of the bull)

From the car park at Kate Kearney's Cottage, walk along the track leading into the Gap of Dunloe. A notice board on the right offers advice to walkers. Turn right at this point to follow a good zig-zag track uphill. This can be boggy in places, but is mostly grassy and avoids steep, roughly vegetated slopes. Unfortunately, it dumps walkers at some old turf cuttings, where progress further southwards can be difficult. Forge onwards, trying to avoid the worst bogs, eventually gaining firmer ground on the lower slopes of Cnoc an Bhráca. You could climb this mountain first, but I'd suggest contouring round its flanks to reach a gap on the other side. From the gap, head up a stony slope to reach the summit of Cnoc na dTarbh. Large upended blocks of rock mark the point.

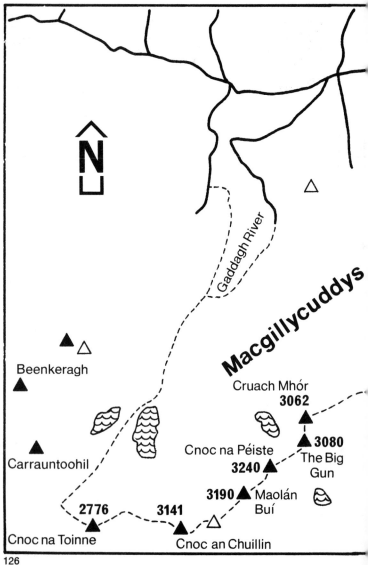

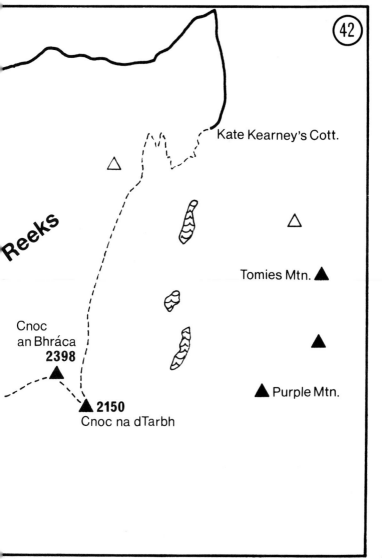

Kate Kearney's Cott.

Reeks

Tomies Mtn. ▲

Cnoc
an Bhráca
2398
▲

▲ **2150**
Cnoc na dTarbh

▲ Purple Mtn.

Cnoc an Bhráca (cnoc an bhráca = speckled hill)
Walk back down to the gap below Cnoc na dTarbh, then head straight up the steep, rugged slope of Cnoc an Bhráca. The summit is marked with a tall cairn and carries a line of posts.

Cruach Mhór (cruach mhór = big steep-sided mountain)
Walk along the broad crest of Cnoc an Bhráca, crossing a minor rise before descending to a gap. A path leads the whole way, later rising towards Cruach Mhór by zig-zagging up a steep, heathery, rocky slope. There are a couple of level stages on this ascent, which are useful places to stop for a breather. The summit ridge is mounted with a huge wall-like structure which has a niche to hold a small statue.

The Big Gun
On leaving the summit of Cruach Mhór, the ridge-walk immediately runs into difficulties. Chaotic heaps of rock are followed by some exposed scrambling where hands will have to be used. Many sharp pinnacles can be by-passed by using well-trodden lines, but experienced scramblers may wish to include a few difficult moves. A final pull leads up to the rocky summit of The Big Gun.

Cnoc na Péiste (cnoc na péiste = hill of the serpent)
A rocky ridge leads down to a gap which is fairly easy to negotiate. The ridge rising to Cnoc na Péiste, however, is far too rocky for most walkers to tackle direct. Outflank it by keeping to the left. The way forwards is still quite difficult, but eventually a final steep climb leads to the summit of Cnoc na Péiste.

Maolán Buí (maolán buí = little yellow hill)
Difficulties end on the summit of Cnoc na Péiste and a simple, largely grassy ridge walk leads across a gap and up to the summit of Maolán Buí.

Cnoc an Chuillinn (cnoc an chuillinn = hill of the slope)
A stony, but gentle descent gives way to a grassy ridge. Most of the ridge is fairly level, but there is a rise along the way which some walkers may wish to treat as a separate summit. I don't think it qualifies, but others may feel that its great height of 3,038ft (926m) offsets any other failings it may have. It doesn't really matter - we're crossing it anyway! Keep

Macgillycuddy's Reeks - a long ridge of 3,000ft summits

going along the ridge for a gentle ascent to the grassy summit of Cnoc an Chuillinn, which is marked with a cairn.

Cnoc na Toinne (cnoc na toinne = hill of the back)
A lengthier descent than any yet encountered along the Reeks ridge leads down stony slopes to a grassy gap. Climb uphill, passing through a ruined fence. At the top of this slope is a gentle rise, but this isn't the true summit. Keep walking along the grassy ridge, but not even the main summit is marked in any special way.

Descend via the gentle, grassy ridge, which steepens to reach the next low gap. Ahead is the great cone of Carrauntoohil, but our day's walk is largely over. Exit to the right, heading down the damp, bouldery gully called the Devil's Ladder. Take care not to dislodge boulders, as these are all quite loose. At the foot of the gully, set a course between two loughs and ford the stream flowing from Lough Gouragh. Walk gently downhill, following a clear track parallel to the Gaddagh River. The track leads down to a network of minor roads and there isn't really an alternative to the road-walk back to Kate Kearney's Cottage. You can, however, cut a corner from the roads by fording the Gaddagh River and following a track and minor road on the opposite side. If you can arrange to be picked up by someone, then you can save walking the last few miles. Kate Kearney's Cottage is, incidentally, a pub - so you've something to aim for!

Alternatives:

Tough and experienced walkers with bags of time and energy to spare can link this walk with Walk 41, adding Carrauntoohil and its satellites to the traverse of the Reeks ridge. It's also possible to cover the Reeks summits from the Black Valley. This is a shorter walk, but involves much steeper, rougher ascents and descents. You can reach the first summit - Cnoc na dTarbh - from the Gap of Dunloe. At the end, instead of descending via the Devil's Ladder, pick a way carefully down the steep, grassy slopes to Curraghmore Lake. Whichever options are chosen, there's no way of avoiding the rocky scramble along the ridge, but you can do yourself a favour and save the walk for a clear, dry day.

WALK 43:

Summits:	Tomies Mountain	2,413ft (735m)	V 895868
	Tomies South Top	2,480ft (757m)	V 894858
	Shehy Mountain	2,503ft (762m)	V 902857
	Purple Mountain	2,739ft (832m)	V 887852

Character:	A tough walk over four mountain summits poised between the Gap of Dunloe and the Lakes of Killarney.
Distance:	11 miles (18 kilometres).
Maps:	1:50,000 Sheet 78. Half Inch Sheets 20 or 21.
	1:25,000 Sheets - Macgillycuddy's Reeks & Killarney National Park.
Start/Finish:	Kate Kearney's Cottage.
Getting There:	Kate Kearney's Cottage is on the way to the Gap of Dunloe and is reached from Killarney or Killorglin via Fossa or Beaufort.

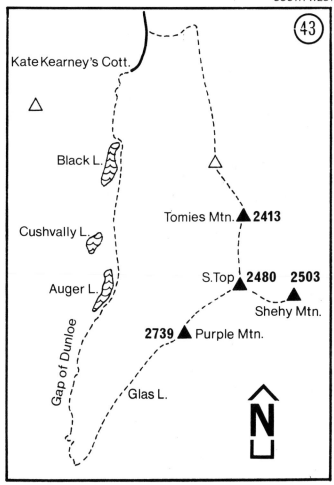

Kate Kearney's Cott.

Black L.

Cushvally L.

Auger L.

Gap of Dunloe

Glas L.

Tomies Mtn. ▲ 2413

S.Top ▲ 2480   2503 ▲ Shehy Mtn.

2739 ▲ Purple Mtn.

N

THE ROUTE

Tomies Mountain (tóimí = mounds)
From Kate Kearney's Cottage, head back down the tarmac road, crossing a river before making a right turn along a track. This can be

131

rather wet and muddy, but it finally gives access to the rugged slopes of Tomies. The heathery slopes gradually steepen and there is no path to follow. The uphill slog eases at a subsidiary summit bearing a cairn. There is a vague sort of path onwards, leading up the next slope where the heather is gradually replaced by stones. The whole top of Tomies is stony, with a few cairns around the summit. Views along the Reeks ridge are very good.

Tomies South Top
A simple walk southwards leads to this subsidiary summit after crossing a broad, stony gap. In mist, don't be confused by a rocky hump sitting in the middle of the gap.

Shehy Mountain
An easy walk south-eastwards leads across a broad, stony gap. There are a few cairns marking the route. From the summit of Shehy Mountain there is a good view over the Lakes of Killarney.

Purple Mountain
Retrace your steps to Tomies South Top, then walk south-westwards, following a path along the main ridge to reach Purple Mountain. The stony summit is marked with a cairn.

Descents in most directions lead into rough or dangerous country. The safest descent lies south-westwards, charting a course across rocky, heathery slopes to reach the tiny Glas Lough. This is the key to the descent. Next, follow a ruined wall downhill, roughly parallel to the stream outflowing from the lough. A ruined fence later heads off to the right and leads walkers safely to the head of the Gap of Dunloe. Simply turn right to follow the broad track through the Gap. This is a remarkably scenic walk, and the jarveys with their horses and jaunting cars do their best to keep motorists at bay. As you walk past frowning cliffs and lovely loughs, there are a couple of places where you can break for a pot of tea. Kate Kearney's Cottage, back at the start of the walk, is a pub.

Alternatives:
There aren't really any worth considering. All other lines of ascent tend to be steep and rugged. Descents other than the one described could be dangerous. On no account try to descend directly into the Gap of Dunloe as unseen cliffs are very difficult to outflank.

WALK 44:

Summits:	Caherconree	2,713ft (826m)	Q 732073
	Baurtregaum	2,796ft (851m)	Q 750077

Character: Two fine summits crowning the Slieve Mish Mountains. Both the start and finish of the walk use waymarked paths.

Distance: 11 miles (18 kilometres).

Maps: 1:50,000 Sheet 71. Half Inch Sheet 20.

Start/Finish: Beheenagh.

Getting There: Beheenagh is on a minor road between Camp and Aughils, reached via the R559 or R561 roads respectively.

THE ROUTE

Caherconree (cathair Chonraoí = fort of Cu Roi Mac Daire)
Signposts indicating Caherconree point the way along the minor road between Camp and Aughils. There is a small lay-by near Beheenagh and a notice board indicates a waymarked path. Simply follow the red and white marker posts across boggy slopes. The ground steepens towards the head of this desolate glen, but firmer footing is found as height is gained. On reaching a high gap, turn left and continue to trace a rather sparser line of marker posts. This could be awkward in mist as you'd lose sight of one before seeing the next in line. Cu Roi Mac Daire - the magical, mythical King of Munster - would frequently confound his enemies with sudden descents of mist! The markers lead to a huge wall - the remains of a prehistoric promontory fort attributed to the hands of Cu Roi Mac Daire. This site is well worth exploring and is in a fine state of preservation. Continue uphill, without the benefit of markers, on grassy and stony slopes. Eventually, a steep edge can be followed to a broad summit bearing a cairn.

Baurtregaum (barr trí gcúm = top of the three hollows)
Keep to the steep edge of Caherconree, which descends to become a narrow, grassy ridge leading down to a broad, stony gap. The ascent of Baurtregaum crosses stony slopes bearing occasional grassy patches. The top of the mountain is broad and stony, but has a summit trig point,

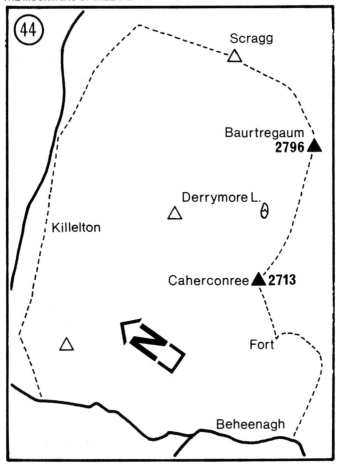

several cairns and some crude shelters.

Descend by walking north-eastwards, following a broad crest. Later, correct course by heading northwards, crossing a subsidiary hump before descending on steep, rugged ground. The well blazed Dingle Way will eventually be reached and the walking becomes easier. Keen summit baggers might feel that the walk should have included Gearhane and Glanbrack Mountain, but I don't think they really count as separate summits. The Dingle Way leads towards some modern buildings, then passes the ruins of Killelton village. Yellow markers show the way along a series of tracks, but the Dingle Way is abandoned near Camp. A left turn leads up a narrow minor road to return to the lay-by near Beheenagh.

Alternatives:

If you're really pining to tick off Gearhane and Glanbrack Mountain, then you could construct a circuit from Killelton to include those minor summits along with Caherconree and Baurtregaum. There is perhaps no finer expedition on the Dingle Peninsula than a complete east to west traverse over all the main mountains. I therefore suggest that hardy mountain walkers might link Walks 44, 45, 46 and 47.

WALK 45:

Summits:	Stradbally Mountain	2,627ft (798m)	Q 587092
	Beenoskee	2,713ft (826m)	Q 581089
	Coumbaun	2,017ft (610m)	Q 568092
Character:	Two fine mountains and one rather dull lump rising from the coastal plain above Stradbally.		
Distance:	10 miles (16 kilometres).		
Maps:	1:50,000 Sheets 70 & 71. Half Inch Sheet 20.		
Start/Finish:	Stradbally.		
Getting There:	Stradbally is on a minor road between Camp and Brandon. It can also be reached from Dingle via the Connor Pass.		

THE ROUTE

Stradbally Mountain

Walk eastwards along the road from Stradbally to reach the junction for Killiney. Opposite this "T" junction is a track leading into a forest. Walk into the forest, following the track uphill, then take a left turn at a junction. Later, walk uphill on boggy ground following the forest fence. As the slope steepens it becomes bouldery and heathery. A stony ridge finally leads to the top of the mountain - a stony dome with a summit cairn.

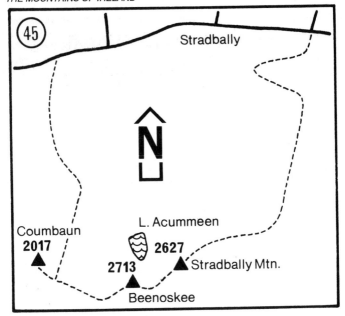

Beenoskee (binn os gaoith = mountain over the wind)
A stony slope leads down to a stony gap overlooking a small lough. A grassier slope, which is still rather stony, leads up to the top of Beenoskee. There is a broken trig point on the summit, alongside a cairn. Views take in all the mountains of the Dingle peninsula, as well as those further afield on the Iveragh peninsula.

Coumbaun (cúm bán = white hollow)
A long, stony slope with some grassy patches eventually leads down to a gap of stones and peat hags. In mist, care should be exercised on this descent, as it's easy for walkers to be drawn off course and be most of the way to Anascaul before realising. From the gap, however, a short, easy, grassy slope leads up to a tiny summit cairn.

Return to the gap, then descend steeply northwards. Follow a stream at first, but look ahead for a track on the right-hand side. This can be followed downhill for a while, then a direct line can be taken to reach a farm. The farm stands by a minor road and a right turn leads back to Stradbally and its two pubs.

Clouds catch the summit of Beenoskee

Alternatives:
Instead of returning to Stradbally, you could descend southwards from
Coumbaun, crossing a broad and bleak gap to link with Walk 46.

WALK 46:

Summits:	Slievanea	2,026ft (620m)	Q 508057
	Slievanea North Top	2,200ft (670m)	Q 516063
	Gowlanebeg	2,134ft (649m)	Q 522046
	Banoge North	2,094ft (641m)	Q 548048

Character:	Four fairly easy summits between the Connor Pass and Anascaul.
Distance:	11 miles (18 kilometres).
Maps:	1:50,000 Sheet 70. Half Inch Sheet 20.
Start:	Connor Pass.
Finish:	Anascaul.
Getting There:	The Connor Pass is crossed by a minor road running from Dingle to Stradbally. Anascaul is on the R559 road between Camp and Dingle.

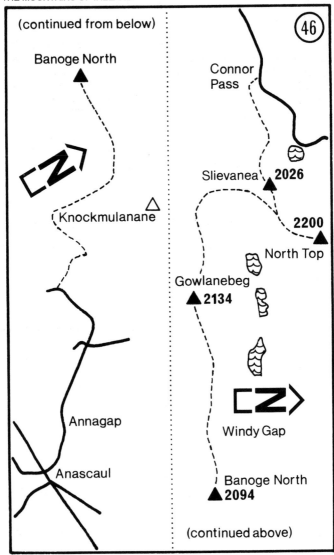

(continued from below)

46

Banoge North

Connor
Pass

Slievanea **2026**

Knockmulanane

2200
North Top

Gowlanebeg
2134

CZ>

Windy Gap

Annagap

Anascaul

Banoge North
2094

(continued above)

THE ROUTE
Slievanea

Starting from the top of the Connor Pass, there is a track running uphill opposite the car park. Follow this for only a short way, then climb more steeply uphill to the left. A stone banking can be traced around the edge of a cliff from a shelter. The shelter may at first appear to mark the summit, but the true summit is further around the curve of the cliff edge.

Slievanea North Top

Keep near the cliff edge, enjoying fine views across the Connor Pass towards Brandon Mountain. Cross a gentle, peaty gap, then climb uphill to reach a smooth, rounded, grassy summit.

Gowlanebeg

Return to the peaty gap, then bear left to contour along the slopes of Slievanea to reach a wide gap between Slievanea and Croaghskearda. The gap is stony, with peat hags. You could follow a rocky ridge southwards to reach the summit of Croaghskearda, but I haven't given this point a separate listing. After looking at it long and hard I felt it didn't quite make the grade. To continue to the next summit, climb uphill to reach a stony area. There is a summit trig point and a cairn.

Banoge North

Head roughly eastwards to descend to the Windy Gap. In mist, take care over the exact line, especially when a stream tends to pull you towards a dangerous cliff-line. Once across the deep gap, climb a steep, heathery slope. This reaches a cairn on a spur of the mountain. Walk further along to pass a prominent rocky knob on the shoulder of the mountain. The summit is a short way beyond - a stony place bearing a cairn.

Descend westwards to reach a narrow, heathery ridge. Walk along the ridge, then contour around the southern slopes of Knockmulanane. This is all rugged ground, but a fence can be followed down to join a clear track. The track zig-zags down to a huddle of farm buildings on a narrow road. Turn left to follow the road to a crossroads, then go straight through the crossroads to reach Anascaul. The village has shops and pubs.

Alternatives:

You could climb two of these summits from Anascaul, and two from the

Connor Pass. It's also possible to start early from Anascaul and continue across the Connor Pass towards Brandon Mountain. Approaches can also be made from the northern slopes, taking in some lovely loughs in rather bleak surroundings.

WALK 47:

Summits:	Ballysitteragh	2,050ft (624m)	Q 461057
	Brandon Peak	2,764ft (841m)	Q 472095
	Brandon Mountain	3,127ft (952m)	Q 460116
	Masatiompan	2,509ft (763m)	Q 465145

Character:	A rugged ridge-walk over four mountain summits, taking in spectacular scenery throughout. Brandon Mountain is notoriously misty, but try and reserve it for a clear day.
Distance:	12½ miles (20 kilometres).
Maps:	1:50,000 Sheet 70. Half Inch Sheet 20.
Start:	Connor Pass.
Finish:	Tiduff.
Getting There:	The Connor Pass is crossed by a minor road running from Dingle to Stradbally. Tiduff is at the end of a minor road and is signposted for Mount Brandon.

THE ROUTE

Ballysitteragh

Start walking uphill on the same side of the Connor Pass as the car park. A fence can be followed over the first rise, which is called Beenduff. Cross a gap, then climb more steeply alongside a line of fenceposts on Beenabrack. There is a slight gap, then a final grassy rise leads to the summit cairn on Ballysitteragh.

Brandon Peak

A steep slope leads down from Ballysitteragh, then a fence can be followed across a low gap. The fence runs up to a junction of fences on a broad shoulder of Brandon Peak. From this junction, a fence continues up a steepening slope of grass to reach a tiny summit. Some walkers

Summit furniture on Brandon Mountain

may consider that Brandon Peak has two summits, but I discount this first one. Walk along a very narrow, grassy ridge, which becomes a little broader and rockier as the main part of Brandon Peak is reached. A final pull up the rocky peak reaches the summit cairn.

Brandon Mountain (cnoc Bhreandáin = Brendan's hill)
A steep, rocky slope leads down from Brandon Peak, then a narrow, rocky edge can be followed towards Brandon Mountain. There's also a wall and fence just a little downhill from the rocky edge, which some walkers would prefer to follow. The scenery is less impressive, but in mist the wall offers a sure guide. Either way, a steep climb finally leads to the top of the mountain. The summit furniture includes a trig point, cairn, metal cross, ruined oratory and a holy well. Views are exceptionally good, especially of nearby features. The mountains of the Dingle peninsula head off inland, while across Dingle Bay are the mountains of the Iveragh Peninsula. More distant mountains could be discerned on a really clear day.

Masatiompan (más an tiompáin = low hill of the drum)
The ridge running northwards from Brandon Mountain descends in

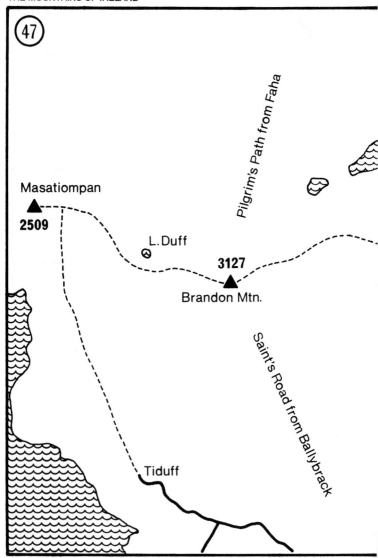

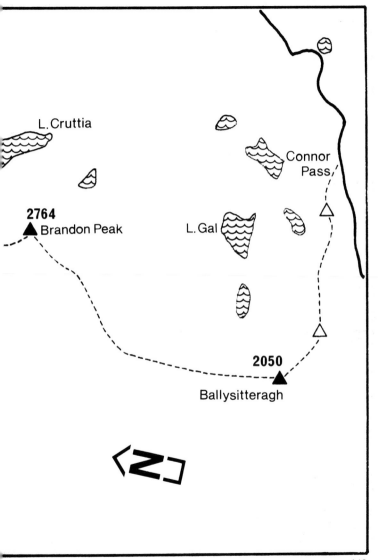

L. Cruttia

2764
▲ Brandon Peak

L. Gal

Connor
Pass

2050
▲
Ballysitteragh

⟨Z⟩

stages, finally crossing the line of the Dingle Way on a gap where an ogham stone stands. There is also a pile of rubble which was once a signal tower. Although sited strategically on the gap, the ever-present mists meant that signals simply couldn't be seen! Climb the slopes ahead, which start off steep and rocky, but become gentler later. The broad summit area is a mixture of moss and stones, crowned with a cairn.

Return to the gap, taking careful aim if the day is misty. From the gap, the Dingle Way offers a waymarked descent in either direction. The easiest route is westwards, following the remains of a broad track associated with the construction of the signal tower. This is generally a grassy line across rugged slopes and although it can be wet in places it's a better route than any other. The lower part of the track is less clear, but the waymarks show the way down a rugged, moorland slope to reach a stony track. This leads down to farmhouses at Tiduff. It's a good idea to arrange to be collected at this point, as it's really too far to walk back to the Connor Pass.

Alternatives:

There are other approaches to Brandon Mountain - nearly all signposted Mount Brandon/Cnoc Bhreandáin in the area. A route known as the Saint's Road is rather vague these days, but can be traced uphill from Ballybrack. There's another pilgrim's path rising from Faha, marked by posts and ending on steep rock. Scramblers can make sport on the ridge running east from the summit of Brandon Mountain. Brandon Peak can be ascended by using a zig-zag track from the road-end at Lough Gal. For a long expedition across the mountains of the Dingle peninsula, forge links between Walks 44, 45, 46 & 47. This is a fine traverse which ends overlooking the Atlantic Ocean, where all the mountains of the south-west ultimately dip their feet.

WEST
37 Mountains - 11 Walks

On the west side of Ireland, the mountains are loosely grouped around Westport. In Connemara there are the Twelve Bens and the Maum Turks - both ranges offering long, hard walks. Smaller groups of mountains lead towards the massive bulk of Mweelrea, then the shapely peak of Croagh Patrick rises - attractive, aloof and apart. Northwards of Westport, a road leads out to Achill Island, where there are two fine mountains. The other group of mountains in this part of the country is the Nephins - forbiddingly remote mountains with a couple of lofty outliers. Geologically, the mountains are a mixed bunch, but are mostly metamorphics. The underlying rock has been subjected to great heat and pressure which has altered its form. Quartzites are common, giving rise to bright, bald, stony mountains. Between the mountains are immense bogs and lonely loughs.

Connemara is beautiful and the tiny Connemara National Park has been established on the Twelve Bens. Although the mountains are exceptionally rugged, they have attracted walkers for some time and general access is very good. The Maum Turks offer a gruelling bogtrot along their length - if you can't do it in one go you'll have to carry a tent for use half-way. Mighty Mweelrea is difficult to approach from all sides, being guarded by the sea, sheer cliffs and barren bogs. By way of complete contrast, Croagh Patrick has a wide, well-blazed pilgrim path up to its summit chapel. In North Mayo, however, you should prepare for the worst. The long, hard walk through the Nephin Beg Range isn't easy to complete in a day - you may have to take a tent with you. The full traverse of the range will one day be recognised as one of Ireland's classic walks, but few walkers tackle it at the moment. The only Irish mountains to be found on an island are located in this area - two fine mountains overlooking the Atlantic on Achill Island.

PADDY'S WAY - WEST

It was late summer when I returned to complete my tour of the mountains of Ireland. I made Benlettery Youth Hostel my base for a couple of nights. I completed a circuit of the Twelve Bens in a day and hoped I would be

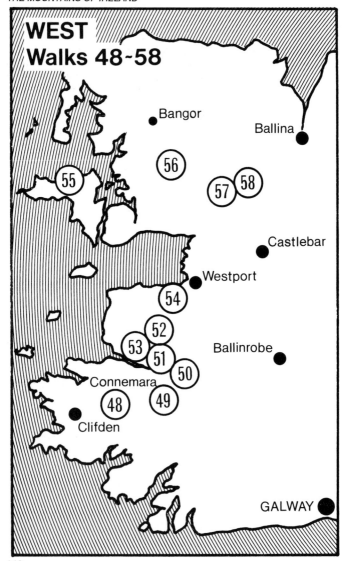

WEST
Walks 48~58

Bangor

Ballina

55

56

57 58

Castlebar

Westport

54

52

53

51

50

Ballinrobe

Connemara

48 49

Clifden

GALWAY

able to complete the traverse of the Maum Turks in a day too. However, a late start and poor weather meant that I had to pitch my tent half-way along the range. Handy B&Bs helped me through smaller groups of mountains on my way towards Mweelrea. I spent the night in a tin hut so that I could rise early and beat the plagues of midges which rose like a mist above the bogs. I set off in moonlight towards Mweelrea, but the midges got me before I reached the breezy summit. As I started early, I thought I might as well head for Croagh Patrick the same day. I was given a lift there by an athletic Swiss climber who also wanted to make a summit bid. I found an Independent Hostel to recover in afterwards!

I used an Independent Hostel after climbing the two big mountains on Achill Island, then composed myself for the great trek through the Nephin Beg Range. I made a late start, so couldn't have hoped to complete the walk in a day. I made sure I pitched my tent on the highest summit to beat the evening mist of midges. The Nephins rise from a vast bogland where the midges can be particularly bad - no-one walked the streets in the village of Bangor! I stayed in another Independent Hostel, then decided to tackle Bireencorragh and Nephin together. The midges certainly kept me on my toes - I found that if I walked briskly they couldn't get me. I was exhausted by the time I got a lift to the youth hostel at Westport.

WALK 48:

Summits:	Derryclare	2,220ft (677m)	L 815510
	Bencorr	2,336ft (712m)	L 811522
	Bencollaghduff	2,290ft (698m)	L 798530
	Benbreen	2,276ft (694m)	L 783515
	Bengower	2,184ft (666m)	L 782506
	Benbaun	2,395ft (730m)	L 785540
	Benfree	2,065ft (630m)	L 777544
	Muckanaght	2,153ft (656m)	L 768541
	Bencullagh	2,084ft (635m)	L 756537
Character:	A circuit of the Twelve Bens of Connemara, though in this case there are only nine summits. This is an arduous walk combining two horseshoe routes, crossing rugged terrain.		
Distance:	20 miles (32 kilometres).		

Maps:	1:50,000 Sheets 38 & 45. Half Inch Sheets 10 or 11.
	1:50,000 Sheet - Mountains of Connemara (not an OS publication).
Start/Finish:	Benlettery Youth Hostel.
Getting There:	Benlettery Youth Hostel is on the main N59 road between Recess and Clifden.

THE ROUTE

Derryclare (binn dhoire chláir = mountain of the oakwood of the plain)
From the youth hostel, follow the main N59 road in the direction of Recess, then take a narrow road on the left to enter Glencoaghan. This road crosses a river, passes a few buildings, then runs across the rugged flank of Derryclare. Branch off to the right at any point, later picking up a trodden path up a heathery shoulder. As height is gained, the ground becomes rockier. There are a number of false summits along the way, but the main one bears a cairn.

Bencorr (binn chorr = mountain of the rounded hill)
Walk roughly northwards along a rocky, hummocky ridge to descend to a gap. A rocky, bouldery slope leads up to the summit cairn on Bencorr.

Bencollaghduff (binn dubh = black mountain)
In mist, take care to follow the correct route down from Bencorr. Walk along the ridge, but not too far, then branch off left to descend a steep and rocky slope. There are gravelly paths leading down to a gap. The gap is a strip of peaty grass flanked by two rock walls. You'll probably have to use your hands to get across, but it's not a major obstacle. A long pull up a rocky slope leads to the summit cairn on Bencollaghduff.

Benbreen (binn bhraoin = mountain of the drop)
Walk down a steep, rocky ridge, avoiding awkward outcrops by following trodden paths. A final rockface before the broad, rocky gap needs care. Outflank it on the left-hand side, then walk down to the gap. A long climb up a broad, rocky ridge leads to a series of rocky humps and bumps. These can all be outflanked, if you're in a hurry, or you can visit them all, if you're an ardent summit-bagger. In mist they have the appearance of false summits, but eventually you'll reach the cairn on the main summit.

Bengower (binn gabhair = mountain of the goat)
A steep, scree-covered slope leads southwards from the summit of Benbreen. This can be "run" by those who know how to, but if you don't then pick a way down the side of it. After crossing a low, rocky gap, the face of Bengower looks unassailable. Locate a route up a series of gullies and terraces. You'll need to use your hands, but you'll probably agree that the climb isn't as tough as it looked from the bottom. A short walk leads across the top to the summit cairn. If the effort so far has been too much, or if you're simply running out of time, then you can head straight off the end of the ridge for a steep, rugged descent to Benlettery Youth Hostel.

Benbaun (binn bhán = white mountain)
You probably won't be able to remember the intricacies of the ascent of Bengower, so you could find it entertaining to try and reverse the route. Somehow, return to the gap, then climb back to the summit of Benbreen. If you "ran" down the scree, you'll find it much slower work struggling back up the side of it. Once across the summit, you have to walk back over all the subsidiary humps and bumps to return to a distant gap. Once on the gap, bear left across a rocky slope to reach the lowest gap of the whole walk - Maumina. From this point, Benbaun's bulk looks unattractive. Steep, grassy slopes lead up to a narrow band of rock, so you'll have to find a way through this obstacle. It's not difficult, and once through there is an easy walk up a grassy ridge to reach the stony summit. There is a trig point and cairn. This is the highest point in Co Galway and views range across the mountains of Connemara, embracing bleak bogs, loughs, sea inlets, islands and so on. It's a very involved view which takes some sorting out if you've plenty of time and a good map.

Benfree (binn fhraoigh = mountain of heather)
A ridge of rock and scree descending from Benbaun becomes grassy as it leads down to a gap. A short walk uphill from the gap leads to the summit of Benfree.

Muckanaght (meacanagh = place of lumps and ridges)
Steep, grassy slopes lead down from Benfree to a peaty gap. Steep, grassy slopes then lead uphill from the gap, becoming rockier towards the top of the mountain. There is a cairn on the summit.

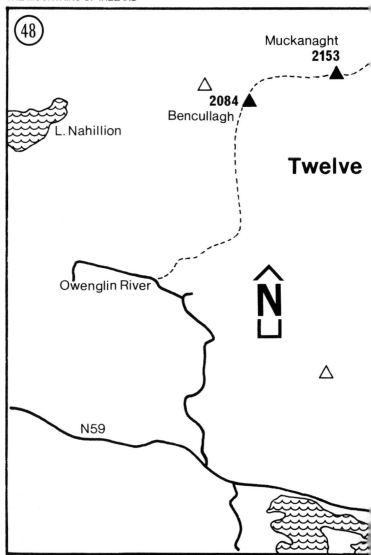

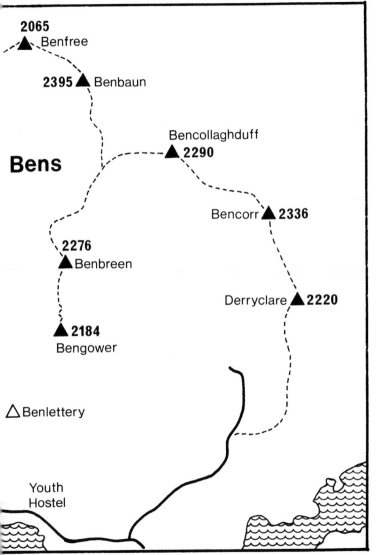

2065
▲ Benfree

2395 ▲ Benbaun

Bencollaghduff
▲ **2290**

Bens

Bencorr ▲ **2336**

2276
▲ Benbreen

Derryclare ▲ **2220**

▲ **2184**
Bengower

△ Benlettery

Youth
Hostel

Bencullagh (binn na chailleach = mountain of the old woman)
A gentler slope leads down to the next gap, and the uphill walk isn't too steep either. The vegetation changes from grass to heather, but the top of Bencullagh is stony. Some walkers might feel obliged to include a subsidiary summit a little further westwards, but it doesn't really merit a separate listing.

Descend southwards over rock, scree and moorland, following a stream down to a forest. This is hard work, but once the forest is reached, you can turn right and pick up a good track. This leads through the forest and emerges to join a minor road. Turn left to follow the road over a broad moorland rise, then descend through a forested area to reach the main N59 road. Turn left to follow the main road back to Benlettery Youth Hostel.

Alternatives:
The walk can be split into two horseshoe routes - both of which can be based on the youth hostel. Benbaun, being a prominent mountain, is sometimes climbed purely for its own sake. This can be done from the head of either Glencorbet or Gleninagh. Approaches to the Twelve Bens can also be made from the Connemara National Park, via Diamond Hill, or from the road serving the TV mast on Cregg.

WALK 49:

Summits:	Corcogemore	2,012ft (613m)	L 952492
	Mullach Glas	2,045ft (624m)	L 937493
	Binn Mhór	2,174ft (663m)	L 918494
	Binn Chaonaigh	2,076ft (633m)	L 912515
	Binn idir an Dá Log	2,307ft (703m)	L 888529
	Letterbreckaun	2,193ft (669m)	L 856551
	Leenaun Hill	2,052ft (625m)	L 874593
Character:	Seven summits ranged along the Maum Turks Mountains. These can be covered in a single, long, hard walk, but the route is not recommended in mist.		
Distance:	20 miles (32 kilometres).		
Maps:	1:50,000 Sheets 38 & 45. Half Inch Sheets 10 or 11.		
	1:50,000 Sheet - Mountains of Connemara (not an OS publication).		

Start:	Near Maumwee Lough.
Finish:	Leenaun.
Getting There:	Maumwee Lough is on a minor road between Maam Cross and Maum. Leenaun is on the main N59 road between Clifden and Westport.

THE ROUTE

Corcogemore

Start near the top of the minor road between Maam Cross and Maum. There is a small lay-by beside the road and a walk westwards leads across a small area of turf cuttings. Pick up the line of a fence and follow this uphill. It twists and turns on a rocky, boggy slope and has some steep sections, but it offers a sure guide to the upper parts of the mountain. A summit cairn stands in an area of hummocky, rocky ground.

Mullach Glas (mullach glas = grey summit)

Walk north-west across unmarked hummocky ground, then descend more steeply westwards to reach a gap of rock and heather. A steep climb up a rocky, heathery spur follows, then a line of fenceposts can be traced across the top of the mountain, running fairly close to the summit.

Binn Mhór (binn mhór = big mountain)

Follow the line of fenceposts only a little way downhill, then bear right to descend to a gap. A short walk up from the gap leads to a complex area of rocky humps and pools. Keep to the broad crest of the mountain to reach the summit trig point.

Binn Chaonaigh (binn chaonach = mountain of moss)

Take care on the descent from Binn Mhór to avoid steep, rocky slopes. There is no problem in clear weather to find the low gap of Maumeen, but in mist it's easy to go astray and there are nasty cliffs in most directions. Try to keep to ground which looks vaguely trodden, though even this line is a steep, rocky descent. Eventually, a fence can be followed out onto the gap, but it's best to keep above it to contour around the slopes of a boggy hump sitting astride the gap. A pilgrim path crosses Maumeen to reach a chapel, holy well and Stations of the Cross. Climb steeply uphill from the chapel, later following a fence. Towards the top of the mountain, branch away from the fence to reach the summit cairn in a rocky area.

153

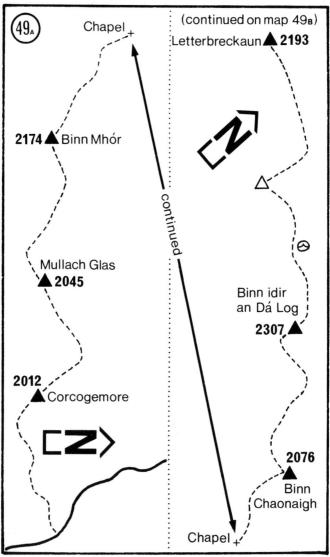

(49ₐ)

Chapel +

(continued on map 49ʙ)

Letterbreckaun ▲ 2193

2174 ▲ Binn Mhór

continued

Mullach Glas
▲ 2045

Binn idir
an Dá Log

2307 ▲

2012
▲ Corcogemore

2076
▲
Binn
Chaonaigh

Chapel +

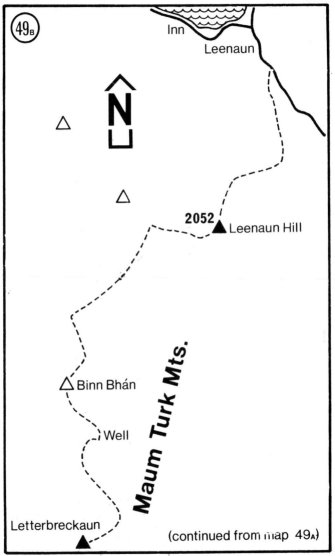

49ᴮ

Inn

Leenaun

2052 ▲ Leenaun Hill

Maum Turk Mts.

△ Binn Bhán

Well

Letterbreckaun ▲

(continued from map 49ᴀ)

Binn idir an Dá Log (binn idir an dá loch = mountain between two lakes)
Paths can be found trodden into the scree on the descent from Binn
Chaonaigh. After crossing a wide gap, there are other trodden paths
which can be used to outflank a series of rocky, boggy, humps and
bumps. It's a complex ridge, involving marked changes of direction, but
in clear weather it should present no problems. Avoid all the minor
summits and steer a course towards the main summit cairn - which is the
highest point along the Maum Turk Mountains.

Letterbreckaun

Trodden paths lead down from the summit of Binn idir an Dá Log. The
slope is gradual at first, then becomes steeper and could prove awkward
in mist. There is a cliff-line guarding the way to the gap of Mam Ochóige
and it needs to be outflanked carefully on one side or the other. The gap
itself is quite complicated, having a series of hillocks and a small lough.
A steep, heathery ascent from the gap runs into rocky patches. The
gradient eases a little above this, and the intermediate summit of
Knocknahullion is crossed. Turn sharply northwards to descend, then
follow a rugged ridge of humps, bumps and pools. This ridge runs into
a series of rocky ribs which provide a route onto Letterbreckaun. The
rocky, bouldery top of the mountain bears cairns in addition to the one
on the summit.

Leenaun Hill

There is a long walk over a handful of intermediate summits between
Letterbreckaun and Leenaun Hill. Start with an awkward descent from
Letterbreckaun, with changes of direction and a steep rockface being
encountered on the way to the low gap of Maum Turk. A steep climb
leads up from the gap, then a fence can be followed over Binn Bhán.
Turn right at a junction of fences to descend to a broad, low, boggy gap.
Follow the fence uphill from the gap, turning right at the top. The fence
follows a grassy ridge, then we must bear left, leaving the fence to cross
a broad, stony, peaty moor. The summit of Leenaun Hill is marked with
a cairn.

The classic Maum Turks Walk doesn't visit Leenaun Hill, but heads
off for a descent to the Leenaun Inn. Our final ascent calls for a slightly
different ending. Head northwards to pick up a ridge. Follow this until it
suddenly steepens, then turn right to walk down a steep slope to reach
a stream. Cross the stream and follow a clear track downhill to a road.

Turn left to follow the road into Leenaun, where there are shops and pubs.

Alternatives:
This long, hard walk can be split into shorter walks. Leenaun Hill, for instance, is rather out on a limb and could be climbed for its own sake from Leenaun. The other summits are perhaps best covered in two groups of three, using the pilgrim path as an access route for both walks. The problem lies in making circular walks to return to Maumeen, though there are tracks and minor roads which could be pressed into service for this purpose. Whatever options are chosen, save all your walking in the Maum Turks Mountains for clear, dry days, when you can see where you are going and enjoy the rough walking.

WALK 50:

Summits:	Maumtrasna	2,239ft (681m)	L 962637
	Devilsmother	2,131ft (648m)	L 916624
Character:	A plateau-like summit connected to another summit by a rugged ridge-walk, with a steep ascent and descent.		
Distance:	10 miles (16 kilometres).		
Maps:	1:50,000 Sheets 37 & 38. Half Inch Sheets 10 or 11.		
Start/Finish:	Glennacally Bridge.		
Getting There:	Glennacally Bridge is on the main N59 road between Leenaun and Westport.		

THE ROUTE

Maumtrasna (mám trasna = pass across)
Start from Glennacally Bridge, on the opposite side of the bridge to a B&B. There is a gate in the fence by the road, then it's simply a matter of following the river upstream. The way is rugged, featuring bog, bog-oak and boulders. Cross a tributary stream, then bear left to climb an immense spur of the distant Maumtrasna. This spur becomes steeper as height is gained, then the slope eases after passing a prominent outcrop of rock. Keep walking along a broad crest, which runs into the

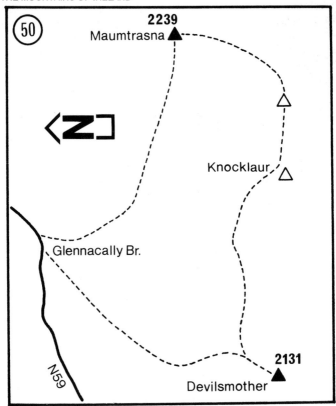

extensive summit plateau of Maumtrasna. This is a desolate area, featuring much bare rock interspersed with areas of bog or standing water. In clear weather you could wander all over this fascinating area, but in mist you'd be advised to stick to your map and compass. Pick the likeliest looking summit, as there are odd cairns and high crests scattered around. The vast, sprawling shoulders of the plateau have slight rises which very keen summit-baggers might feel inclined to visit, but they don't really count as separate mountain summits.

The ever-popular Gap of Dunloe and its magnificent scenery (Walk 43)
Brandon Peak, clearing nicely on a fine evening (Walk 47)

A distant evening view of the Twelve Bens across Killary Harbour (Walk 48)
Looking down on Doo Lough from the steep slopes of Ben Creggan (Walk 51)

Devilsmother (binn gharbh = rough mountain)
Head roughly southwards off the vast plateau, swinging gradually westwards to cross boggy and bouldery areas. There is a slight ascent over a hump of moorland - not really a separate summit - then a gradual descent along a rugged ridge punctuated with a couple of minor bumps. A steeper descent finally leads down to a low gap with narrow sides. The ridge climbs towards Devilsmother, at first following a fence. As the ground begins to level out, another broad ridge joins from the right and both pursue a common course to the top of the mountain. There are twin summits, both bearing cairns and having fine views of all the mountains of Connemara and ranges on both sides of Killary Harbour's great inlet.

Retrace steps slightly, then walk down the broad ridge to its end. A sudden, steep, and rather rough descent returns walkers to Glennacally Bridge.

Alternatives:
A circuit of these two mountains could also be constructed from Lough Nafooey, using the long, rugged ridges on the southern side of the mountain. It's also possible to walk the steep ridge between the summit of Devilsmother and the roadside near Aasleagh Falls.

WALK 51:

Summits:	Ben Creggan	2,283ft (695m)	L 857666
	Ben Creggan South Top	2,200ft (670m)	L 858661
	Ben Gorm	2,303ft (701m)	L 862652
Character:	Three summits perched above very steep, rocky slopes.		
Distance:	4 miles (6 kilometres).		
Maps:	1:50,000 Sheet 37. Half Inch Sheets 10 or 11.		
Start/Finish:	Doo Lough.		
Getting There:	Doo Lough is on the R335 road between Aasleagh Falls and Louisburgh.		

THE ROUTE

Ben Creggan (binn cruachán = steep-sided mountain)
Start from the shores of Doo Lough, where the Liscarney road branches

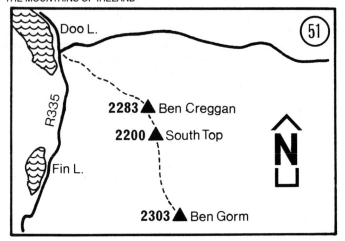

from the R335 road. Ben Creggan looks practically unassailable and frowns on humble walkers. Obviously, care must be exercised on the ascent. The idea is to pick a way up steep lines of grass between rocky outcrops. The gradient is punishing, but by keeping to the right-hand side of the rugged ridge, most obstacles can be by-passed fairly easily. As you pause to catch your breath at intervals, splendid views unfold of Mweelrea. When the steep slope finally eases, the summit cairn is only a short walk onwards.

Ben Creggan South Top

A simple walk down a grassy and rocky slope leads to a gap. A walk uphill from the gap quickly leads to the subsidiary summit.

Ben Gorm (binn gorm = blue mountain)

Walk down another grassy and rocky slope to reach a gap. Walk uphill to reach the summit cairn on Ben Gorm. There is another cairn nearby. The top of Ben Gorm is fairly broad, with peaty and stony areas. Return to Doo Lough by carefully retracing your steps.

Alternatives:

A less steep and rocky descent could be made along the gentler ridge leading towards Aasleagh Falls. Follow this ridge until a fence offers a straight line down to the falls. It's also possible to complete a circular route over the three summits by following fairly easy ridges from Tawnyard Lough. The walk over these summits is hard work, but fairly short. If you find you still have plenty of time and energy to spare you could walk over the nearby Sheefry Hills too.

WALK 52:

Summits:	Sheefry Hills West Top	2,500ft (760m)	L 848695
	Sheefry Hills	2,504ft (761m)	L 861695
	Sheefry Hills East Top	2,429ft (739m)	L 883708
Character:	Very steep ascent and descent, but an easy walk over the three summits of the Sheefry Hills.		
Distance:	9 miles (14 kilometres).		
Maps:	1:50,000 Sheet 37. Half Inch Sheets 10 or 11.		
Start/Finish:	Doo Lough.		
Getting There:	Doo Lough is on the R335 road between Aasleagh Falls and Louisburgh.		

THE ROUTE

Sheefry Hills West Top
Start at the junction of the R335 road with the minor road signposted for Liscarney. Follow the Liscarney road only a short way, then ford the river running parallel to it. Exceedingly steep and difficult grass slopes lead upwards, requiring considerable effort. Minor rocky outcrops are easily by-passed, but frequent pauses will be needed to catch your breath. Eventually, the steep slopes ease and a broad, stony top is reached. There is a summit cairn and views over nearby mountains feature quite rugged slopes.

Sheefry Hills
Follow a narrow, grassy ridge, crossing a minor rise before reaching the summit trig point in the middle of the Sheefry Hills. The trig point is being used as a straining post to hold a wire fence taut!

Sheefry Hills East Top
Continue along the broad crest of the Sheefry Hills, crossing another

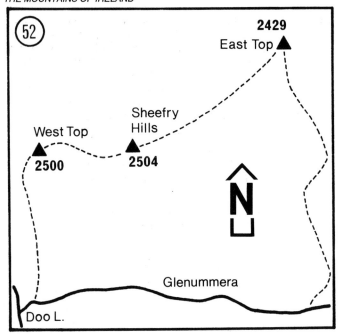

minor rise before descending to a shallow gap. Walk uphill, looking around to settle on the highest part of this last rise. There is a small cairn which seems to mark the summit.

Follow a broad, stony ridge south-westwards for the descent. The ridge steepens and becomes narrower, reaching a peaty gap. Turn right to descend a very steep slope from the gap. Avoid a line of rocky outcrops by threading a way between them, then continue down into a boggy valley. Follow a stream down the valley, delighting in some little waterfalls, then follow a track past a farm. Turn right to follow a minor road back to the shores of Doo Lough.

Alternatives:
If you've enough time and energy left you could set off straight up the rugged end of Ben Creggan to reach Ben Gorm, but it's very hard work.

WALK 53:

Summits:	Mweelrea	2,688ft (818m)	L 790668
	Ben Bury	2,610ft (794m)	L 802683
	Ben Lugmore	2,616ft (796m)	L 815672

Character: Three mountain summits which are fairly easy to link, but whose approach routes are quite soul-destroying. This is a fine group of mountains, best reserved for a clear day.

Distance: 10 miles (16 kilometres).

Maps: 1:50,000 Sheet 37. Half Inch Sheets 10 or 11.

Start/Finish: Delphi Adventure Centre.

Getting There: Delphi Adventure Centre is on the R335 road between Aasleagh Falls and Louisburgh.

THE ROUTE

Mweelrea (maol riabhach = bald grey hill)

Walk out onto the boggy moorland at the back of the Delphi Adventure Centre. A path runs alongside a fence, then is later confined to a boggy strip of tussocky grass between the fence and a river. The fence encloses a forestry plantation, and once clear of this, it's possible to take any line across a broad, boggy area of grass. This is all difficult, tussocky stuff, with Mweelrea rising nearby, yet never seeming to draw nearer. The ascent starts from the level, boggy grassland and you should aim for the ridge well to the left of Mweelrea. Follow a stream uphill at first, then bear left from it to reach a gap on the ridge. Although the ascent is steep, the ground becomes easier to walk as height is gained and a path can be followed. The path stays close to the edge of a cliff for the final pull up to the summit. There is a cairn on the peaty top and it's worth recording that this is the highest point in both Co Mayo and the Province of Connacht. Views take in the mountains of Connemara across the inlet of Killary Harbour, plus many more distant ranges throughout the west of Ireland.

Ben Bury

Descend via the grassy and stony slopes leading roughly north-eastwards from the summit of Mweelrea. There are some exposed rocky slabs, but

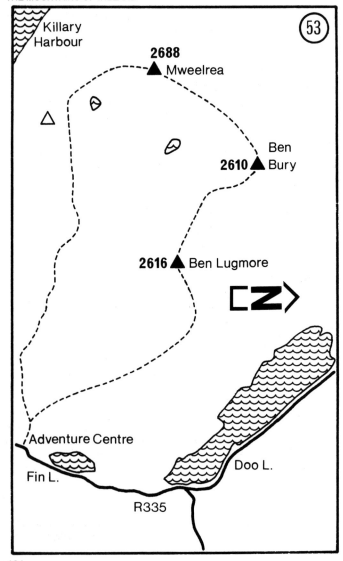

these are set at easy angles. Cross a broad gap, then walk up a rugged slope. The ground begins to level out and becomes quite stony. A number of cairns mark false summits - the true summit cairn being reached in a bouldery area.

Ben Lugmore (binn log mhór = mountain of the big hollow)
Walk south-eastwards to descend to a gap overlooking a tremendous hollow on the mountainside. Climb up to a prominent peak and follow a ridge poised over an impressive cliff-line. Some walkers may feel that Ben Lugmore should be credited with two, or even three separate summits, but I'm only offering one. As we're crossing the entire ridge, you can tick off any extras if you really feel that they count.

Eventually, the ridge begins to fall and you should bear right to pick up a steep, rugged spur of the mountain. This takes walkers down to a broad, boggy area with much tussocky grass. Forge across this awkward patch of country, hopefully arriving at a river which can be crossed by way of a rather shaky looking log and rope bridge. This structure, if it still exists, will have been noticed on the outward journey. Once across the river, turn left to follow the boggy path alongside the fence to return to the Delphi Adventure Centre. There is a cafe on site, if you need anything to eat or drink.

Alternatives:
There are no easy routes on Mweelrea - let's be quite clear about that - though a number of routes could be attempted. The shortest involves crossing Killary Harbour from the youth hostel, for which you need to organise some sort of ferry. The steep, rugged slopes are purgatorial, so you're only saving on distance. A narrow shore path can be followed from Bundorragha, along the side of Killary Harbour, ending with a steep, rugged ascent to Mweelrea. Any of the steep, rocky spurs rising above Delphi could be attempted - they are all hard work and some routes involve scrambling. Another scrambler's ascent makes its way up the vast hollow between Ben Bury and Ben Lugmore. Finally, you could try and ascend from the north-west climbing on steep, tussocky grass slopes. Plenty of choices, but no easy routes!

WALK 54:

Summit:	Croagh Patrick	2,510ft (764m) L 906801
Character:	A stony slog up a pilgrim path to reach a summit chapel. If you do this one according to certain "rules" you can gain some everlasting benefit for your soul!	
Distance:	5 miles (8 kilometres).	
Maps:	1:50,000 Sheets 30 & 31. Half Inch Sheets 10 or 11.	
Start/Finish:	Murrisk.	
Getting There:	Murrisk is on the R335 road between Westport and Louisburgh.	

THE ROUTE

Croagh Patrick (cruach Phádraig = Patrick's steep-sided mountain)
A large car park is available at Murrisk, but it can be crowded. A narrow road leads to a statue of St Patrick and a notice lists the "rules" which must be observed if you're to gain any spiritual benefit from the climb. Walk uphill on the broad, stony, overtrodden path. This leads up the heathery slopes of the mountain. There will usually be other people

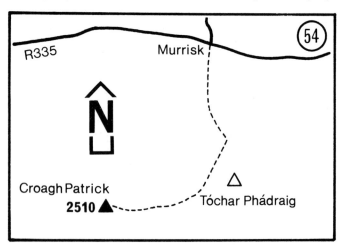

around, which is most unusual on Irish mountains. Anyone with a stick is almost certainly Irish, but not all Irish people carry sticks! Most European nationalities are represented on a good Summer day, with Americans and Australians also showing an interest. Huge crowds are present on the last Sunday in July, if you want to avoid that date! There is a level stretch of path around the half-way mark, with toilets available. After this brief interlude, the mountain rears up and walkers follow a river of boulders almost to the top of Croagh Patrick. The last short stretch is easy and leads to the summit chapel and toilets. The relative aloofness and isolation of Croagh Patrick makes it a fine viewpoint, enabling mountain ranges throughout the west of Ireland to be studied. Clew Bay, at the foot of the mountain, is also worth a mention - it's supposed to have one island for every day of the year, if you've time to check them all! If you're following the "rules", then you've got to visit a site on the far side of the mountain. If, however, you're here simply for the sake of ticking off this lofty summit, then walk back down to Murrisk. There's a pub and ruined abbey you might want to visit before leaving.

Alternatives:
The ascent described is the modern pilgrimage route, or at least "modern" in the sense that there was an earlier line. The older route, which was trodden by St Patrick, has been re-opened in recent years and is known as the Tóchar Phádraig. It starts at Ballintubber Abbey and offers a 22 mile (35 kilometre) route to the summit of Croagh Patrick. Every step features some legend or story, which adds to the interest of the route. If you can spare the time for it, this is a fine route to Ireland's Holy Mountain.

WALK 55:

Summits:	Slievemore	2,204ft (671m)	F 650087
	Croaghaun	2,200ft (670m)	F 560060
Character:	Two fine mountain summits high above the Atlantic - and the only Irish mountains to be found on an island.		
Distance:	10 miles (16 kilometres).		
Maps:	1:50,000 Sheets 22 or 30. Half Inch Sheet 6.		
Start:	Doogort.		

Finish:　　　　Keem Strand.

Getting There:　Doogort and Keem Strand are reached by minor roads around the north and west of Achill Island.

THE ROUTE

Slievemore (sliabh mhór = big mountain)
There's no doubting Slievemore - it positively looms over holidaymakers at Doogort. Follow the minor road past the Strand Hotel, then start walking uphill as soon as there is a way off the road. The ground is boggy and pathless at first. Aim for a prominent ridge and a path will eventually be found rising through the heather. Slievemore is heathery from top to toe, though boulders become more apparent as height is gained. After negotiating a rockstep on the rocky ridge, the way ahead is predominantly rocky. Stay on the ridge, then after a final uphill stretch a fairly level walk leads to the summit trig point and cairn shelter.

Croaghaun (cruachán = steep sided mountain)
Walk down from the summit of Slievemore, heading roughly westwards past boulders, heather and a wide, boggy area. On the next part of the descent, a rockstep is encountered, but it is easily outflanked. After that, it's best to swing southwards, aiming for the deserted village of Slievemore. Turn right at those grey, roofless ruins and follow a broad track gradually uphill. After passing above a quarry, climb onto the moorland crest and aim for a ruined tower on a low hill. Continue along the broad, moorland crest, crossing rugged, boggy ground before the lengthy uphill struggle onto Croaghaun. As height is gained the intricate, colourful, shattered cliff-line above the Atlantic can be studied in detail. Beware of crumbling edges, noting that some deep fissures are opening up in places. A final bouldery climb leads to the summit cairn. This is the highest point on Croaghaun, though there is a subsidiary summit further along which sports a finer peak of rock. Both are worth a visit, but I haven't given the second one a separate listing.

Descend a steep slope towards Keem Strand. The heathery slopes turn out to be easier to descend than they might first appear. It's still rather tough going in places. The road-end can be seen at Keem Strand, but it's perhaps better to cross a small stream and bear left to pick up the road at a higher level, just above a series of zig-zags. Its useful if you've arranged for someone to come and meet you on the road, as it's a long walk to the nearest village.

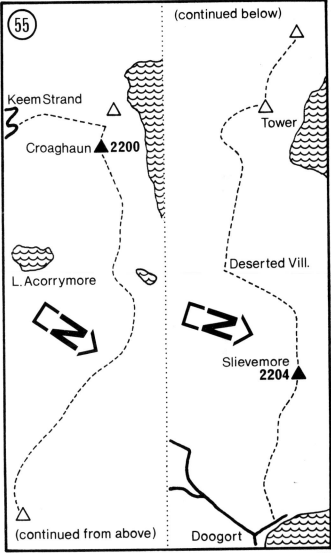

Alternatives:

Both Slievemore and Croaghaun can be climbed on separate occasions to make two shorter walks. It's also interesting to continue from Croaghaun to Achill Head, scrambling along an airy crest of rock above the sea. Apart from these two heights, walkers staying on Achill Island also tend to visit the Menawn Cliffs.

WALK 56:

Summits:	Corranabinnia			
	South Top	2,200ft (670m)	F	895026
	Corranabinnia	2,343ft (713m)	F	903032
	Glennamong	2,067ft (629m)	F	913057
	Nephin Beg	2,065ft (628m)	F	932102
	Slieve Cor	2,396ft (721m)	F	915145

Character:	A long, hard walk through very remote country covering the five summits of the Nephin Beg Range. Clear weather is a definite advantage for this traverse.
Distance:	24 miles (39 kilometres).
Maps:	1:50,000 Sheets 23, 30 & 31. Half Inch Sheet 6.
Start:	Glendahurk Bridge.
Finish:	Bangor.
Getting There:	Both the start and finish of the walk are on the main N59 road west and north of Newport.

THE ROUTE

Corranabinnia South Top

It can be awkward to locate the start of this walk. When travelling along the main N59 road west of Newport, there are many narrow minor roads branching northwards. Most are simply drives to farms or houses, but the turning for Glendahurk Bridge is marked with a small, battered sign reading "Carheenbrack". The narrow tarmac road becomes a stony track before reaching Glendahurk Bridge. Pass a few old buildings in a clump of trees, then follow a broad bog road uphill. Branch right from this track at any point to pick a way up a broad, boggy, heathery slope. There are some odd boulders around, then a vague path can be traced over a broad rise. Rocky outcrops are passed in a grassier area, then a steep climb leads to the grassy top of the mountain. A very small cairn marks the summit. Directly northwards, the ground falls into a rough, bouldery coum.

Corranabinnia (coire na binne = hollow of the mountain)
A fairly narrow ridge leads downhill, poised above the bouldery coum. Fangs of rock can be by-passed, though the use of hands may be required in odd places. After crossing the gap, an ascent leads up to a stony area. The summit of Corranabinnia is marked with a trig point and a cairn.

Glennamong (gleann na mhóin = glen of the bog)
Walk downhill to a gap which has the appearance of a blunt ridge. An ascent from the gap leads across areas of peat and stones, with some large boulders being encountered. A final pull leads up to the summit cairn. Walkers will begin to appreciate the scale of the vast boglands which surround the Nephin Beg Range.

Nephin Beg
Descend north-westwards from Glennamong. A series of slopes separated by more level areas lead downhill. The ground is boggy, heathery and grassy. Aim to cross a stream, then climb up to an old track. We're not following the track anywhere, but simply crossing it and following a steep, grassy, stony slope up to a minor summit. (In desperation, you could use the track to exit towards Traenlaur Lodge Youth Hostel.) From the minor summit, walk roughly northwards to cross a gap. An ascent leads onto a gentler shoulder of Nephin Beg, where the ground levels out for a while. A final rise is mounted to reach the summit cairn.

Slieve Cor (sliabh cor = round mountain)
Descend north-westwards from Nephin Beg to reach a steep, rugged slope which later levels out. The remains of an electric fence can be traced along a short ridge to reach a stream flowing from Scardaun Lough. A steep, corrugated heathery slope leads up to the subsidiary summit of Corslieve. After this difficult ascent there is a level, boggy area to cross. This becomes increasingly stony as height is gained afterwards.

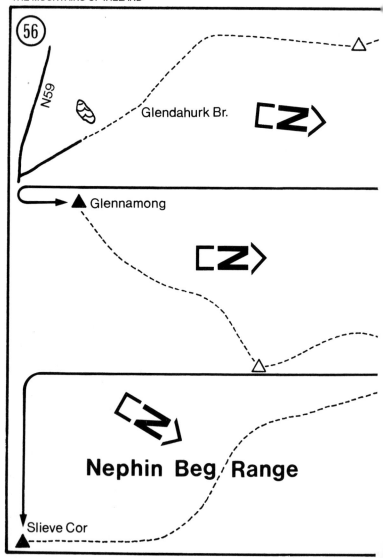

(56)

N59

Glendahurk Br.

[Z〉

▲ Glennamong

[Z〉

△

[Z〉

Nephin Beg Range

Slieve Cor
▲

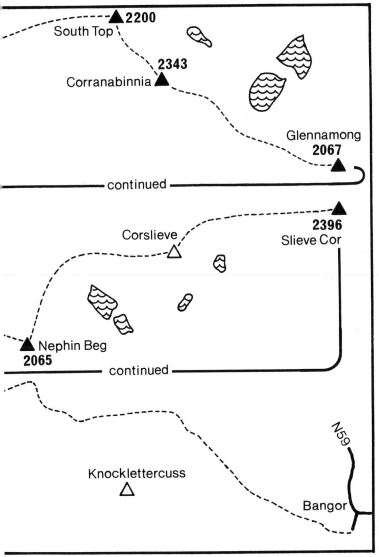

▲**2200**
South Top

2343
Corranabinnia ▲

Glennamong
2067 ▲

— continued —

Corslieve △

▲ **2396**
Slieve Cor

▲ Nephin Beg
2065
— continued —

Knocklettercuss
△

N59

Bangor

173

A gently graded slope leads to the top of the mountain, which is a bouldery area bound by moss. The huge summit cairn is called Laghtdauhybaun and is crowned with a trig point. Views across the broad, empty boglands take in Nephin and the Nephin Beg Range, with other mountains featuring distantly.

This final summit is in the middle of nowhere. There is a lengthy descent yet to come, followed by a lengthy walk-out to Bangor. Start by walking roughly northwards from Slieve Cor, then swing north-westwards to descend more steeply. This line is rough enough, but at the foot of the slope is a level, boggy area sprinkled with pools of water. Avoid the pools and aim to cross two streams to reach an old track on the slopes of a distant hill. The track is falling into disrepair, but still offers a clear line to Bangor. Despite having boggy and overgrown sections, it offers the best means of progress across the flanks of Knocklettercuss. Bangor has shops and pubs, which you may well need after walking through the entire Nephin Beg Range in a single walk.

Alternatives:

The three southern summits of the Nephin Beg Range could be covered in a fairly simple walk from Glendahurk Bridge. The other two summits are rather remote. Slieve Cor could be reached from Bangor purely for its own sake. Nephin Beg is more isolated, but anyone following the old track through the mountains to Bangor could include the summit of Nephin Beg in their plans.

WALK 57:

Summit: .	Birreencorragh 2,295ft (698m) G 025050
Character:	A fairly steep climb to a solitary mountain summit.
Distance:	6 miles (10 kilometres).
Maps:	1:50,000 Sheets 23 or 31. Half Inch Sheet 6.
Start/Finish:	Clendavoolagh Lodge.
Getting There:	A minor road leads to Clendavoolagh Lodge from Keenagh. Keenagh can be reached from Newport, Crossmolina, or from the R312 road.

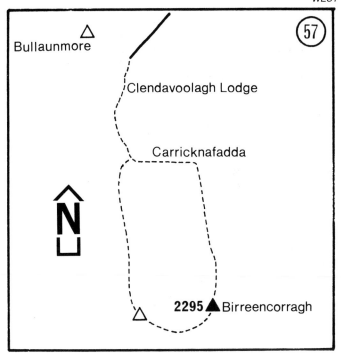

THE ROUTE

Birreencorragh (barrín carraig = rocky little top)

A narrow tarmac road traces a river upstream from Keenagh, ending at Clendavoolagh Lodge. A track continues towards the head of the glen, passing through gates. There are a few ruins, then a solitary cottage at the end of the track. A direct ascent can be made from here, crossing boggy slopes at first, then tackling ever-steepening heather slopes. The final stretch becomes stony and reaches a shoulder of Birreencorragh at some stout, square cairns. Turn right and walk across a slight dip in the broad shoulder. There is heather to the left and stony ground to the right. A steeper ascent is quite stony, but there is more heather on the final walk to the summit trig point. This is a very good viewpoint for studying the Nephin Beg Range, as well as Nephin.

A descent can be made by using a broad ridge leading back down into the glen. A steep slope falls from the summit to reach a gap. After crossing a slight rise beyond the gap, always bearing right, the grass and peat ridge leads gradually downhill. Fences and gates are passed before walkers can regain the track to Clendavoolagh Lodge.

Alternatives:

The route described, either clockwise or anti-clockwise, is about the easiest way of tackling Birreencorragh. Longer walks along more rugged ridges could also be considered. It's also possible for walkers to head off towards Nephin, crossing difficult moorlands before reaching the road between the two mountains.

WALK 58:

Summit:	Nephin	2,646ft (805m) G 104079
Character:	A fairly straightforward walk up a huge, solitary mountain.	
Distance:	5 miles (8 kilometres).	
Maps:	1:50,000 Sheets 23 or 31. Half Inch Sheet 6.	
Start/Finish:	On the south-west side of Nephin.	
Getting There:	The south-west side of Nephin can be reached via the R312 road between Castlebar and Bellacorick, or via the R315 and R316 roads from Crossmolina, or via the R317 road from Newport.	

THE ROUTE

Nephin

When travelling along the R312 road, look out for a forest edge rising up the south-western slopes of Nephin. Follow the forest fence uphill from the roadside. This is fairly difficult at first, but as height is gained and the forest is left behind the walking becomes easier. There is a fence to be crossed before the shoulder of the mountain is reached. Simply keep heading uphill - first along the rugged, heathery, hummocky shoulder, then over some rocky sections. There is a fairly good path in places. Heathery and stony slopes alternate and some cairns on stony brows

The stony northern slopes of Nephin

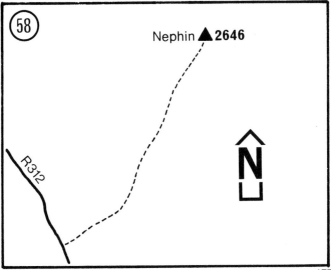

Nephin ▲2646

R312

N

turn out to be false summits. A cairn and shelter are passed before the true summit is reached - which is marked with a trig point. Stony slopes fall northwards and there are remarkable extensive views on a clear day. Walk back down the broad shoulder to return to the roadside near the forest.

Alternatives:
Approaches from any other point are over steeper and rockier ground. You could also enjoy a rugged mini-horseshoe route from the northern side of the mountain.

North - a little word which covers a large area. The mountains in the north of Ireland are concentrated in groups which are often widely spread. Cuilcagh and Truskmore are solitary summits, while the Blue Stack Mountains and the mountains of north-west Donegal are more closely grouped. The latter mountains are close to, or even just inside Glenveagh National Park. A solitary, stony summit rises from a bogland on the Inishowen peninsula, while the Sperrin Mountains are both boggy and stony. That leaves only the Mountains of Mourne - a small and isolated group which boasts of several summits. There is very little which these mountain groups have in common with each other, but I bring them all together in this section. Geologically, they are highly varied, but many of them are huge domes of granite. Cuilcagh and Truskmore feature gritstone plateaus, while Errigal is a shapely peak of quartzite.

Walking in the north is quite popular and you can expect to meet groups of walkers - especially in the Mountains of Mourne, which are handy for Belfast, and in Donegal, which everyone loves. Most of the mountains are easily accessible, but some are quite difficult underfoot. Cuilcagh has a waymarked ascent, but this is notoriously difficult. Truskmore, by contrast, has a road all the way to its summit. Errigal, that gleaming peak in the north-west, is immensely popular. Other mountains tend to be less well walked. There may even be access problems brewing in the Sperrin Mountains. The Ulster Way, in a very roundabout fashion, offers access to many mountain groups. There is the main waymarked circuit around Northern Ireland, then a separate spur leading off through Co Donegal. If you're really determined you could link several groups of mountains by using the Ulster Way.

PADDY'S WAY - NORTH

My late summer tour of the mountains of the west continued into the mountains of the north. It was almost a day's journey from Westport to Florence Court, so I climbed Cuilcagh in the evening and spent the night on the huge summit cairn curled up in my sleeping bag. I came down the

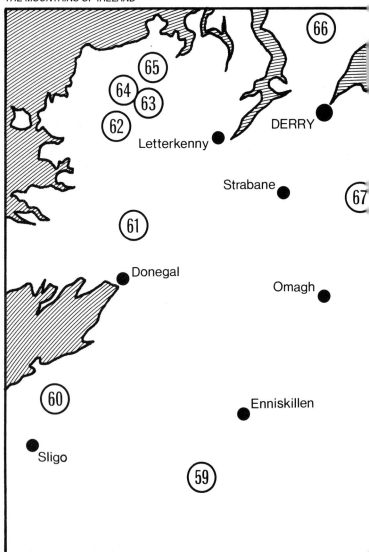

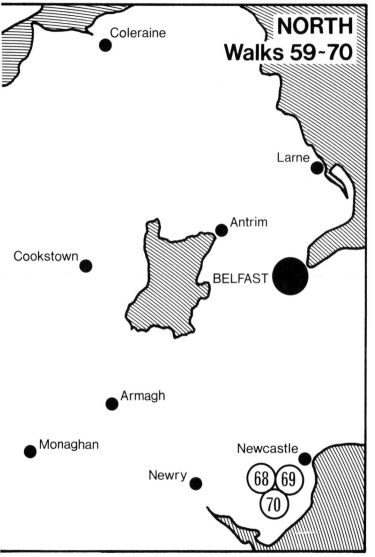

mountain for a good breakfast, then headed for distant Truskmore. I climbed the mountain from Glencar, which is a long way, then came down by road after visiting its subsidiary summit. I stopped for the night at a B&B near the coast. The Blue Stack Mountains were walked the following day and I stopped at another B&B. I moved on to Errigal Youth Hostel, where I intended to base myself for a few days. However, a friend came and whisked me away to his cottage and from there we covered the mountains together.

I continued by myself to finish off the last few mountains in Ireland. Slieve Snaght - the summit in the middle of Inishowen - was easily visited, so I continued to a B&B at Newtownstewart. It sounds like a long day, but I didn't feel rushed when I walked over all the Sperrin Mountains the next day, and got lifts to Belfast Youth Hostel! Only the Mountains of Mourne remained and I was determined to walk them without carrying a heavy pack. I based myself at a B&B at Attical and did all my walking from there. On my final day, I walked from Attical to end at Newcastle Youth Hostel. That was it - I simply ran out of Irish mountains! From Djouce to Donard - I'd done 'em all!

WALK 59:

Summit:	Cuilcagh	2,188ft (665m) H 123280
Character:	An immense moorland shouldering up a bouldery summit. A hard walk on boggy ground following a waymarked path.	
Distance:	12 miles (20 kilometres).	
Maps:	1:50,000 Sheet 26. Half Inch Sheet 7.	
Start/Finish:	Tullyhona, Florence Court.	
Getting There:	Florence Court is off the main A32 road between Enniskillen and Swanlinbar. Tullyhona is a little further along a minor road.	

THE ROUTE

Cuilcagh (cailceach = chalky)
The minor road passing the "big house" at Florence Court goes to Tullyhona. Don't go as far as the roadside church, but turn left up a gravel

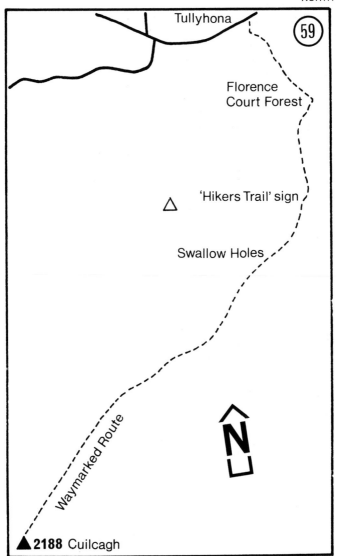

Tullyhona

59

Florence
Court Forest

△ 'Hikers Trail' sign

Swallow Holes

Waymarked Route

N

▲**2188** Cuilcagh

road beforehand. Turn left again, passing a house in the forest, then go through a gate. Turn left yet again and go through another gate. Now turn right to follow another gravel track. Right again takes you up another track which eventually becomes grassy. Don't go through the gate at the end of this track, but turn right one last time to follow a path uphill. This reaches the edge of a forest and a notice reading "Hikers Trail" indicates that the walk is really only just beginning! In theory, it's simply a matter of following a series of yellow marker posts to reach Cuilcagh, but it's a long, hard walk. The posts show the way across a broad limestone area first, passing brackeny areas, bushes and swallow holes. Later, there is a broad, heathery area to cross. Waymarks become rather more spaced apart and in some places it's possible to lose sight of them in mist. On the higher moors, there are a couple of streams to cross. A final steep climb sees a change from tough heather and grass to shorter grass. However, the slope is very steep and there is exposed rock. The summit of Cuilcagh is broad and bouldery, bearing a huge cairn with a trig point perched on top. This is the highest point in both Co Cavan and Co Fermanagh, and although it is an isolated mountain summit it stands in a hilly area. Views can be extensive and the Ordnance Survey once took a sighting from Cuilcagh to Keeper Hill, near Limerick. Providing you leave the summit in the right direction, you'll pick up the waymarks leading back to the forest.

Alternatives:
The waymarked path isn't absolutely foolproof, but it's a fairly good way to reach the summit of Cuilcagh. It's possible to gain some height on minor roads and bog roads, cutting out the early forested sections. Visitors to Marble Arch Caves will find a good track nearby which heads towards Cuilcagh, but ends with miles of unmarked moorlands to be walked. A fine, broad ridge-walk is available from the distant shoulder of Tiltinbane, but first you have to reach Tiltinbane from some point on the western side of the mountain. All these routes are long and hard. The shortest line is from the south, from the Glan Gap on the R200 road. This involves following a forest fence first, then using a broad, boggy crest to reach the higher, rockier parts of Cuilcagh. No route on Cuilcagh can be said to be easy, and clear weather is most helpful.

WALK 60:

Summits:	Truskmore	2,120ft (647m)	G 759473
	Tievebaun	2,007ft (611m)	G 769499

Character: An easy walk linking two summits near Sligo.

Distance: 4 miles (6 kilometres).

Maps: 1:50,000 Sheet 16. Half Inch Sheet 7.

Start/Finish: Truskmore.

Getting There: Truskmore's summit can be reached by road from the scenic Gleniff Horseshoe, which is signposted from the main N15 road between Sligo and Donegal.

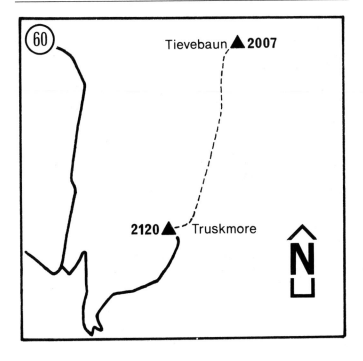

THE ROUTE

Truskmore (trusk mhór = big codfish)
Usually, it's possible to drive up a zig-zag road to reach a tall TV mast on the summit of Truskmore. If the gates at the foot of the road are barred, then simply walk up the road instead. The walk is measured from the summit of Truskmore, which is the highest point in Co Sligo. A point on the slope to the east is the highest point in Co Leitrim. The wide, heathery top of the mountain is stony in places and there are fairly good views of the surrounding hills.

Tievebaun (taobh bhán = white side)
Walk a short way westwards across the broad top of Truskmore, away from the TV mast, then head northwards. A bouldery slope gives way to a gap where level rock is exposed. A low wall continues northward, then a boundary ditch can be traced through a boggy area. An easy ascent is accomplished by following the wall up heathery, bouldery slopes. The top of Tievebaun is quite broad, but the wall, and later a fence, offer a guide across it. It's hard to determine the highest point exactly, but a small cairn may mark it. Turn around and follow the fence, wall, ditch and bouldery slope back to the summit of Truskmore.

Alternatives:

Ascents can be made on any of the rugged slopes rising from Gleniff, Glenade or Glencar. There is a bog-road rising from Glencar which takes walkers half-way to the summit. It's also possible to enjoy a walker's version of the scenic Gleniff Horseshoe, staying on a high level around the glen. This walk could also be amended to include Benbulbin.

WALK 61:

Summits:	Croaghbann	2,100ft (640m)	G 980910
	Ardnageer	2,118ft (644m)	G 971909
	Bluestack	2,219ft (675m)	G 949897
	Lavagh More	2,211ft (672m)	G 945910
	Lavagh Beg	2,100ft (640m)	G 926915
Character:	The five summits of the Blue Stack Mountains vary from being very rocky and difficult to being grassy and easy.		

Distance:	10 miles (16 kilometres).
Maps:	1:50,000 Sheet 11. Half Inch Sheet 3.
Start/Finish:	In the Reelan Valley.
Getting There:	A minor road between Glenties and Ballybofey serves the Reelan Valley and a farm access road reaches the head of the valley.

THE ROUTE

Croaghbann (cruach bhán = white steep sided mountain)
Follow the farm access road towards the head of the Reelan Valley until an old school is reached. Nearby, a farm track leads down to the Reelan River and crosses it. Pass the farm and start climbing the rugged, boggy slopes of Glascarns Hill. Boulders occur more frequently as height is gained. Continue uphill to pass a cairn on a rise, then cross a low gap. The final part of the bouldery ascent reaches a broad top with a pool of water. The summit of Croaghbann is nearby and is marked with a cairn.

Ardnageer (ard na gcaor = height of the berries)
Walk down some exposed slabs of granite and cross some boulders to reach a pool on a gap. The rock scenery is very impressive, but the complex nature of the terrain could make this an awkward area to cross in mist. Looking back, you may wonder how you ever got down from Croaghbann. Looking ahead, you'll have to pick a steep and rocky route, possibly calling for the use of hands. Bouldery ground finally gives way to the summit cairn on Ardnageer.

Blue Stack (cruach gorm = blue steep-sided mountain)
The descent from Ardnageer is followed by a slight reascent on bouldery ground, passing a cairn. This doesn't really count as a separate summit, though some walkers may feel inclined to treat it as one. Nearby is a feature worthy of a short detour - a prominent peak of pure quartz. This is a dazzling landmark on a sunny day (the Irish for quartz is grianchloch = sunstone). Continue down to a boggy, hummocky, rocky gap. A gentle climb uphill is noticeably less rocky than the previous summits. The top of Bluestack is quite broad and more grassy than rocky. There is a summit cairn shelter. Views northwards take in the big mountains around Errigal.

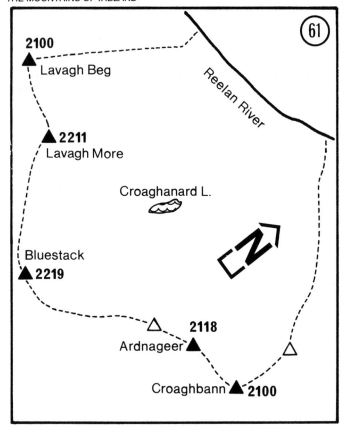

Lavagh More (leamhách mór = big place of elms)
A lengthy descent on grass and boggy ground passes a few boulders
before reaching a gap. Marker posts on the gap show the route of the
Ulster Way as it passes through Co Donegal. A steep, grassy and stony
ascent passes minor rocky outcrops before reaching a broad top. After
weaving between hummocks, the summit cairn will be reached.

Lavagh Beg (leamhách beag = little place of elms)
Walk down to the next grassy gap, then climb uphill mainly on grass. The

progression from bare rock to grass is more or less complete now that we have reached the last of the Blue Stack Mountains. The summit area is hummocky, with a cairn standing between pools of water.

Descend straight down a rugged slope into the Reelan Valley. Look ahead for a bridge and farm access road, then head towards them. As the rugged slope begins to ease, it becomes rather boggy. Cross the bridge over the Reelan River, walk up the access road, then turn right to return to the start of the walk near the old school.

Alternatives:

The approach from the Reelan Valley best lends itself to a circular tour over the Blue Stack Mountains. Walkers who can arrange to be collected elsewhere can make approaches from other points. The Ulster Way has two alternatives which cross the Blue Stack Mountains - offering a choice of routes from the north or south sides of the range. There's also a forest track rising from Letterkillew on the eastern side of the range.

WALK 62:

Summits:	Slieve Snaght	2,240ft (681m) B 923147
Character:	A difficult ascent of a vast, domed mountain.	
Distance:	8 miles (13 kilometres).	
Maps:	1:50,000 Sheet 1. Half Inch Sheet 1.	
Start/Finish:	Dunlewy.	
Getting There:	Dunlewy is reached via the R251 road between Gweedore and Glenveagh National Park.	

THE ROUTE

Slieve Snaght (sliabh sneachta = mountain of snow)
Start from the roofless church at the head of Dunlewy Lough. Go down to the river and find a way across. Walk uphill to cross a rugged rise, then walk upstream alongside the Devlin River. Don't cross the Devlin River, but follow it by using a vaguely trodden path through areas of bog, heather and rocks. Note how the river flows through an attractive cleft where a few trees have managed to find a roothold. After an initial steep ascent, a more level area of bog has to be crossed. After this, follow a tributary stream on the left, climbing steeply up some exposed slabs to

189

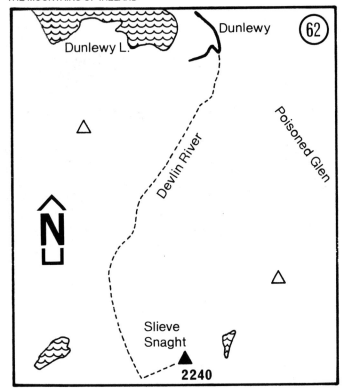

reach a high, bouldery gap. Another left turn leads up an even steeper, rockier slope, where your hands might need to be used. The slope eases later and a simple walk over grass leads to the summit cairn. Care needs to be exercised when retracing your steps to the Devlin River.

Alternatives:
There is a shorter, but steeper rocky ascent following a stream from Lough Barra to the high, bouldery gap. Slieve Snaght can be linked with Dooish, but this involves a long, hard walk through the rocky, boggy Derryveagh Mountains. It's also possible, with care, to include an exploration of the Poisoned Glen, which has impressive boilerplate walls of granite.

Mweelrea - the highest mountain in Connacht (Walk 53)

Croaghaun, Achill Head and the Atlantic Ocean (Walk 55)

Errigal's shapely summit peak, and a fine viewpoint (Walk 64)

Batts Wall leads towards Eagle Mountain (Walk 68)

WALK 63:

Summit:	Dooish	2,147ft (653m) B 983210
Character:	A fairly difficult, but short climb to a bleak summit.	
Distance:	3 miles (5 kilometres).	
Maps:	1:50,000 Sheet 6. Half Inch Sheet 1.	
Start/Finish:	High on the R251 road.	
Getting There:	The highest part of the R251 road can be reached from either Dunlewy or Glenveagh National Park.	

THE ROUTE

Dooish (dubh ais = black back)

Start on the high part of the R251 road, but don't be tempted to head straight for the summit of Dooish as there is an awkward little cliff barring the way. Instead, keep to one or the other side of the summit for the approach. Boggy ground and tussocky grass start immediately you leave the road. After passing beneath an electricity transmission line, a tall deer fence is reached. Stout walkers may have difficulty slipping between the strands of wire, and climbing the thing isn't recommended. The slope beyond gradually steepens and the boggy, heathery ground becomes more bouldery. Pick any line uphill which avoids obvious obstacles. The top of Dooish is a dome of granite and the summit is marked with a cairn. Either retrace steps to the road, or wander down on a slightly different route, but remember the little cliff which rules out a direct descent.

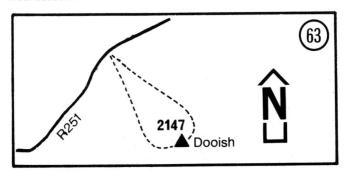

Alternatives:
You could omit the deer fence by making an ascent from Glenveagh, but this is a long, hard walk. It's also possible to follow the broad crest of the Derryveagh Mountains to reach Slieve Snaght, but this is a tough, rocky and boggy walk.

WALK 64:

Summit:	Errigal	2,466ft (750m) B 929207
Character:	A fairly easy, but steep walk to a noble peak.
Distance:	3 miles (5 kilometres).
Maps:	1:50,000 Sheet 1. Half Inch Sheet 1.
Start/Finish:	On the R251 road above Dunlewy.
Getting There:	The R251 road runs between Dunlewy and Glenveagh National Park.

THE ROUTE

Errigal (aireagál = oratory)
There are three trodden routes available to the summit of Errigal from the R251 road above Dunlewy. Two paths are marked with signs and posts, while another starts from a culvert. All these approaches cross boggy, heathery slopes, then reach firmer footing on the shoulder of the mountain. The ridge-walk up the shoulder is steep and rock-strewn, with

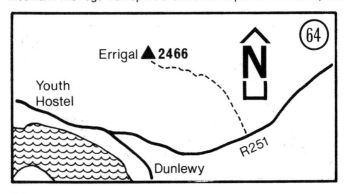

a number of paths trodden into scree. This steep ascent reaches a level area, where a number of cairns include a memorial cairn to Joey Glover (whose knowledge of the mountains of Donegal was unsurpassed). A final, easier walk leads to a neat, pointed summit - an airy perch for studying a view which encompasses most of the north-west of Ireland, including mountains and a heavily indented coastline. This is the highest point in Co Donegal. The usual way to round off the ascent is to walk along a narrow ridge called the "One Man's Pass" to reach a twin summit nearby. Walk back down to the road by reversing the ascent route.

Alternatives:
A direct ascent from Errigal Youth Hostel involves flogging up extensive scree slopes. There's a good route available along the northern ridge. The best walk of all is the "Marathon", which starts from distant Muckish and ends on the summit of Errigal.

WALK 65:

Summit:	Muckish 2,197ft (668m) C 004287
Character:	A steep, fairly easy climb to a rock-strewn summit plateau.
Distance:	4 miles (6 kilometres).
Maps:	1:50,000 Sheet 2. Half Inch Sheet 1.
Start/Finish:	Muckish Gap.
Getting There:	Muckish Gap can be reached via a minor road between Falcarragh and Glenveagh National Park.

THE ROUTE

Muckish (muc ais = back of the pig)
There is a small roadside shrine high on the minor road between Glenveagh National Park and Falcarragh. Behind the shrine is a hummocky, boggy area, then steep ground featuring some minor rocky outcrops. Higher up the slope is a steep, blunt, heathery ridge, which ends with a sudden rash of stones. Walkers continue onto a broad, stony plateau marked with numerous cairns. It can be a confusing area in mist. On a clear day, simply head for a huge cairn, which marks the summit,

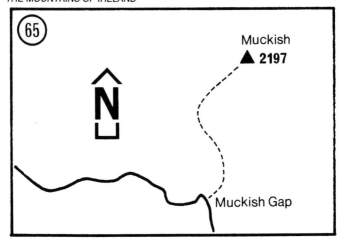

then for a nearby trig point and cross, for a fine view of the edge of the plateau. Turn around and walk back across the plateau and down the ridge to return to the gap.

Alternatives:
Perhaps the most interesting, certainly the most exciting route on the mountain is the Miner's Track on the northern side. This is a steep, zig-zagging track which is falling into disrepair. It offers a close-up view of cliffs and pinnacles on the way to an old quarry, but it wouldn't be to everyone's liking. Muckish is also the starting point for the "Marathon", which crosses boggy Crocknalaragagh, the rounded Aghlas and the rugged Mackoght before ending on the summit of Errigal. It's the best mountain walk in this part of Ireland.

WALK 66:

Summit:	Slieve Snaght 2,019ft (614m) C 423390
Character:	A solitary mountain summit rising from extensive bogs.
Distance:	6 miles (10 kilometres).
Maps:	1:50,000 Sheet 3. Half Inch Sheet 1.

Start/Finish: Lough Fad.

Getting There: Lough Fad is near the R244 road between Buncrana and Carndonagh, with minor road access from Clonmany too.

THE ROUTE

Slieve Snaght (sliabh sneachta = mountain of snow)

There is a "T" junction near Lough Fad. Head away from it in the direction of Carndonagh, then turn right to follow a prominent bog-road. There is some unsightly rubbish dumped along this track, infested with rats, but it leads rapidly across extensive turf cuttings. Keep always to the highest track, which becomes rather rugged before expiring on a slope. There

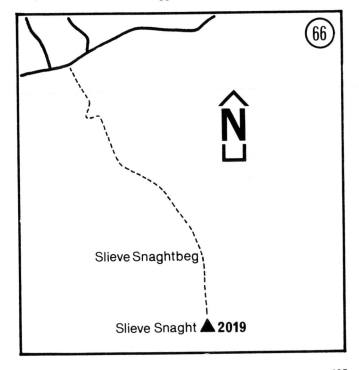

are three parts to this ascent, with level, boggy areas between. This leads to Slieve Snaghtbeg, which has a summit marked with a cairn. Cross a firm, grassy gap beyond, then walk up a bouldery slope to reach the top of Slieve Snaght. This is an area of boulders, with dozens of cairns and small shelters. There is a summit trig point in a walled enclosure. After sampling views over the mountains of Donegal and the distant Sperrin Mountains, turn around and walk back down towards Lough Fad.

Alternatives:
The shortest, boggiest and least inspiring route onto Slieve Snaght starts from a minor road on the eastern side of the mountain. It can hardly be recommended.

WALK 67:

Summits:	Mullaghclogha	2,088ft (635m)	H 557957
	Dart Mountain	2,040ft (619m)	H 602964
	Sawel Mountain	2,240ft (678m)	H 618973
	Meenard Mountain	2,061ft (625m)	H 673986
	Mullaghaneany	2,070ft (627m)	H 685986
Character:	A long, hard walk over boggy, heathery moorland to cover all five summits along the Sperrin Mountains.		
Distance:	22 miles (35 kilometres).		
Maps:	1:50,000 Sheet 13. Half Inch Sheet 4.		
Start/Finish:	Cranagh.		
Getting There:	Cranagh is on the B47 road between Newtownstewart and Draperstown.		

THE ROUTE

Mullaghclogha (mullach cloiche = summit of stones)
From the village of Cranagh, walk in the direction of Plumbridge. The road goes downhill, crosses a bridge, then climbs to Oughtdoorish. Turn right at the farm buildings to follow a gravel track uphill. This passes several fields, then continues through a gate to reach open moorland. After going through another gate, the track becomes overgrown and it's

better to walk uphill alongside a fence. Once above a junction of fences, follow the fence which climbs up through areas which are only a little boggy and rocky. This fairly gentle climb reaches a junction of fences on top of the broad, moorland crest. The summit cairn stands nearby.

Dart Mountain (darta = mountain of the heifers)

Keep walking along the fence, taking care not to trip over loops of rusting wire in the grass and heather. From a corner of the fence, swing gradually north-westwards on the broad, boggy, stony moorland crest. There are minor rises from this rugged crest at Mullaghdoo and Carnakilly - the latter having a rocky edge. Follow a fence by turning left and walking uphill, then turn right and follow a fence downhill. Cross a road at a cattle grid on a low gap in the mountains. Follow a fence uphill from the cattle grid, over a rise, then up a stony moorland slope to reach a cairn on the rocky summit of Dart. The fence ends suddenly at this point.

Sawel Mountain (sabhal = barn)

Descend from Dart, keeping to the broad crest of the Sperrins to cross a broad, peaty gap. Walk up the rounded, grassy slopes of Sawel, where there is very little rock. Cross a fence near the top of the mountain to reach the summit trig point and cairn. This is the highest Sperrin summit and the highest point in both Co Derry and Co Tyrone. Views all round take in the bleak and boggy Sperrins and their accompanying hills. In clear weather you could see from the mountains of Donegal to the Mountains of Mourne.

Meenard Mountain (meán ard = middle height)

A fence is soon joined on the descent from Sawel. There are small areas of bog, followed by some rocky patches. Cross a road at a cattle grid on a low gap in the mountains. Follow a fence uphill to reach a large rock called the County Rock. Continue uphill to cross a minor rise on the heathery moor. The fence runs out later around some heathery humps. A gentle, boggy slope leads to the summit of Meenard Mountain, which is marked by a small cairn.

Mullaghaneany (mullach an eanach = summit of the marsh)

Peaty channels can be avoided on the descent from Meenard Mountain by keeping to the right of the moorland crest. Cross a gap, then walk

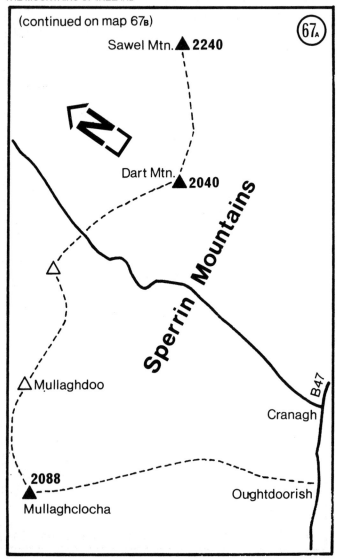

(continued on map 67ʙ)

67ᴀ

Sawel Mtn. ▲ **2240**

N

Dart Mtn. ▲ **2040**

Sperrin Mountains

△

△ Mullaghdoo

B47

Cranagh

2088
▲
Mullaghclocha

Oughtdoorish

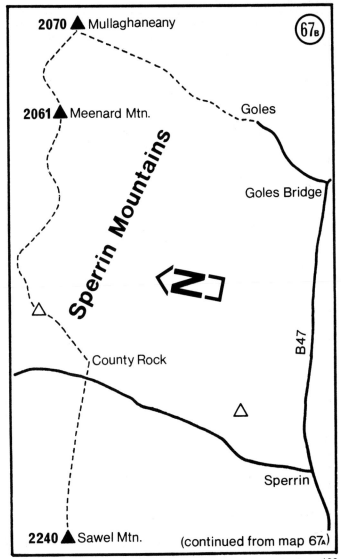

2070 ▲ Mullaghaneany

2061 ▲ Meenard Mtn.

Goles

Goles Bridge

Sperrin Mountains

‹N⌐

B47

△

County Rock

△

Sperrin

2240 ▲ Sawel Mtn.

(continued from map 67ᴀ)

uphill by following firmer patches of grass. A fence crosses the summit and there is a boundary stone inscribed with "LONDONDERRY CORPN BNDRY". This boundary has been traced over all of the five Sperrin summits.

Descend roughly southwards on the broad breast of Mullaghaneany. A track can be picked up low in the valley and this leads to the B47 road at Goles Bridge. Turn right to follow the road back to Cranagh via the village of Sperrin. Many miles of road walking can be avoided if you can arrange to be picked up at Goles Bridge. If you have any time to spare at the end of this long day's walk, then have a look at the Heritage Centre which is reached just before Cranagh.

Alternatives:
This long walk can be split into three easy sections by using the minor roads crossing the Sperrin Mountains near Dart and Sawel. A very long walk can be enjoyed by including a number of minor summits in addition to the five described in the above walk. Follow the moorland crest all the way from Craigagh Hill to Butterlope Glen, staying on the broad crest of the Sperrin Mountains throughout.

WALK 68:

Summits:	Eagle Mountain	2,084ft (638m)	J 244230
	Shanlieve	2,056ft (626m)	J 240227
Character:	Two summits reached by an easy track and a short climb.		
Distance:	8 miles (13 kilometres).		
Maps:	1:50,000 Sheet 29. Half Inch Sheet 9.		
	1:25,000 Sheet - Mourne Country.		
Start/Finish:	Holy Cross Park, Attical.		
Getting There:	Attical lies off the B27 road between Kilkeel and Hilltown. Holy Cross Park is near the village.		

THE ROUTE
Eagle Mountain
Follow a narrow road uphill from Holy Cross Park, passing a waterworks.

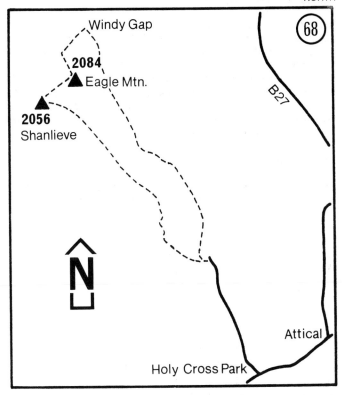

A gravel track leads towards the last building in the valley. Keep to the left of this building, as indicated by signs, then rejoin the track further along. There is a footbridge over a river, but don't cross it. Instead, keep following the track up the valley, staying above the river while tracing it upstream. The track can be rough and stony in places, but it is the most direct line across rugged slopes. A number of side-spurs lead up to small quarries, so don't follow them. Eventually, the track expires at the head of the valley. Turn left to follow a stout wall uphill. The wall turns left, then right. At this point, look out for the small cairn which marks the summit of Eagle Mountain.

Shanlieve (sean sliabh = old mountain)
Simply follow the stout wall across a gritty, bouldery gap and up to a corner. Just off the corner of the wall is the summit cairn of Shanlieve.

Either retrace your steps for the descent, or head roughly south-eastwards to reach the edge of a cliff. This can be rough country, but the scenery is good. As the cliff-line is followed downhill, look out for the remains of an old bog-road. The overgrown zig-zags lead down to the last building in the valley. Turn right to follow the track and road back down to Holy Cross Park.

Alternatives:
Prominent walls can be followed towards these two summits from the Spelga Dam, following the Ulster Way. An ascent can also be made from the Glen River. Hardy mountain walkers could link these two summits with all the summits along the Mourne Wall Walk by heading for Slieve Muck and Walk 70.

WALK 69:

Summits:	Slieve Binnian	2,449ft (747m)	J 320234
	The Back Castles	2,222ft (678m)	J 317245
	Slievelamagan	2,306ft (704m)	J 329260
	Cove Mountain	2,147ft (655m)	J 336271
Character:	Four summits linked by a tough walk in the rugged heart of the Mountains of Mourne.		
Distance:	10 miles (16 kilometres).		
Maps:	1:50,000 Sheet 29. Half Inch Sheet 9.		
	1:25,000 Sheet - Mourne Country.		
Start/Finish:	The Silent Valley.		
Getting There:	The Silent Valley can be reached via minor roads from Annalong, Kilkeel or Attical.		

THE ROUTE
Slieve Binnian (sliabh binnín = mountain of the little peak)
Start the ascent from the tarmac road near the Silent Valley Visitor Centre. A slope of bracken, heather and gorse has to be crossed, then

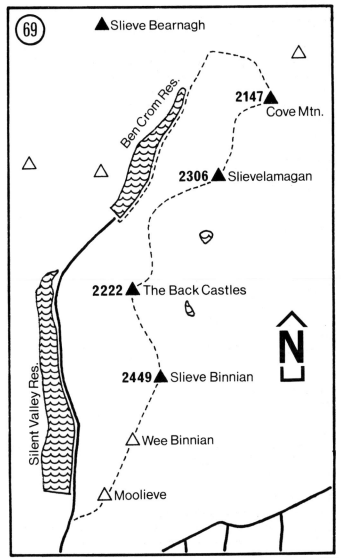

the Mourne Wall is followed over the minor summit of Moolieve. Keep following this stout wall from a junction of walls, heading straight towards Wee Binnian. The upper part of this minor summit is very rocky and is best outflanked on the right. Again, keep following the wall until the rugged slopes of Slieve Binnian become too steep and rocky to support a wall. Pick a careful way uphill between slabs of rock. The top of Slieve Binnian is entirely rocky, reaching a fine summit peak. Views encompass all the main Mountains of Mourne, as well as a considerable stretch of coast.

The Back Castles
The walk along the crest running roughly northwards from Slieve Binnian's summit is quite interesting. Prominent knobs and bosses of rock can either be outflanked or climbed, depending on your ability and inclination. This rugged crest eventually becomes tamer, then a gap is reached. A gentle ascent from the gap leads to a broad, featureless summit. The name of The Back Castles is taken from a series of granite tors nearby, rising awesomely from the shoulder of the mountain.

Slieve Iamagan (sliabh leamháchan = mountain of the little elms)
Head towards the immense Back Castles, then descend to a gap, passing boulders and small outcrops. The gap is an area of rugged moorland. The ascent of Slieve Iamagan is very steep and rough. Boulders, rocky outcrops and heather make it difficult. Eventually, there are rival cairns marking the summit.

Cove Mountain
The descent from Slieve Iamagan starts with a steep, rocky slope, though a vague path might be noticed. After crossing a gap, swing north-eastwards to ascend Cove Mountain. A path traces a rocky edge up to the summit cairn.

The best descent is simply to cross rugged moorlands to the north-west, then walk down steep slopes to reach the Kilkeel River. Turn left to walk above the shores of Ben Crom Reservoir, finally reaching the dam. All that remains is to follow the access road from Ben Crom Reservoir, past the Silent Valley Reservoir, to return to the Visitor Centre. Occasionally, there is a bus service running along the road, so you could shorten the walk. There's also a restaurant near the Visitor Centre, if you're ready for a feed.

Alternatives:
Approaches to these mountains can also be made from the Annalong
River, using the Mourne Wall to ascend Slieve Binnian. After walking
across each of the summits, the walk can be ended by following the
Annalong River back to the start. Walkers with bags of time and energy
to spare could combine a walk over these four summits with a round-up
of the eight summits on Walk 70.

WALK 70:

Summits:	Slieve Muck	2,198ft (674m)	J 281250
	Slieve Loughshannagh	2,030ft (619m)	J 294272
	Slieve Meelbeg	2,310ft (708m)	J 301279
	Slieve Meelmore	2,237ft (680m)	J 306286
	Slieve Bearnagh	2,394ft (739m)	J 313281
	Slieve Commedagh	2,512ft (767m)	J 346286
	Slieve Donard	2,796ft (850m)	J 358277
	Chimney Rock Mountain	2,152ft (656m)	J 364257

Character:	Eight fine summits which are linked by following the Mourne Wall around the Mountains of Mourne. The wall is an excellent guide in mist, but the walk is quite long.
Distance:	20 miles (32 kilometres).
Maps:	1:50,000 Sheet 29. Half Inch Sheet 9.
	1:25,000 Sheet - Mourne Country.
Start/Finish:	Corrigan Bridge.
Getting There:	Corrigan Bridge is near the entrance to the Silent Valley and can be reached from Annalong, Kilkeel or Attical.

THE ROUTE

Slieve Muck (sliabh muc = mountain of the pig)
Walk along the road from Corrigan Bridge in the direction of Attical. Note
the stout wall bounding a forest and follow this away from the road. The
wall leads across a gently sloping moorland, then ends at a junction with
a less well-built wall. A path leads onwards, heading for the bouldery

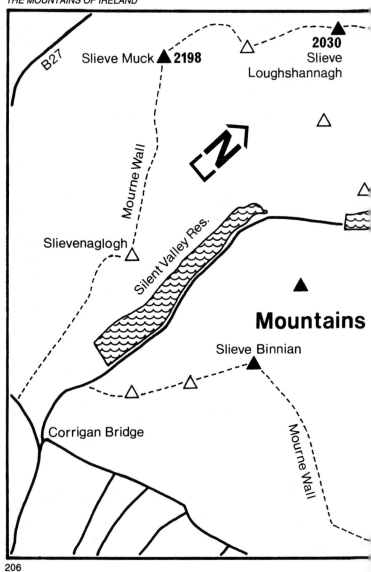

Slieve Muck ▲ **2198**

B27

2030
Slieve
Loughshannagh

Mourne Wall

Slievenaglogh △

Silent Valley Res.

Mountains

Slieve Binnian ▲

Corrigan Bridge

Mourne Wall

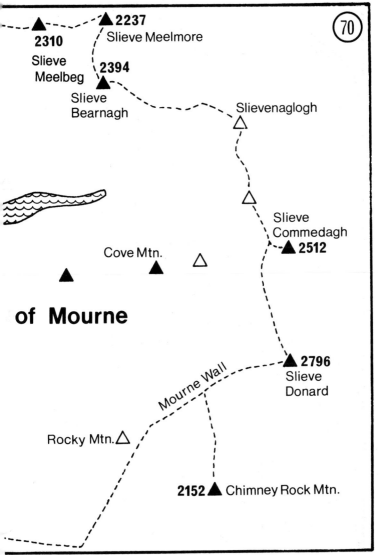

2310
Slieve
Meelbeg

2237
Slieve Meelmore

2394
Slieve
Bearnagh

Slievenaglogh

Slieve
Commedagh
2512

Cove Mtn.

of Mourne

2796
Slieve
Donard

Mourne Wall

Rocky Mtn.

2152 Chimney Rock Mtn.

slopes of Slievenaglogh. Climb over this minor summit, following a wall up, then going down a badly eroded peaty slope. Pass a gateway in the wall, where a track called the Banns Road passes through. Follow the wall up a heathery slope, taking care on a couple of steep, rocky sections. Continue to the grassy top of Slieve Muck, aiming for the summit trig point near a junction of walls.

Slieve Loughshannagh (sliabh loch seana = mountain of the old lake)
Follow the wall running northwards, taking a grassy line from the summit of Slieve Muck to reach a gap. Climb up to the intermediate summit of Carn Mountain by following the wall over its heathery slopes. On the descent from Carn Mountain, the wall assumes the stout proportions of the "real" Mourne Wall. It runs down from Carn Mountain, crosses a minor bump, then runs down to a gap. Climb up a heathery slope, following the wall to the summit of Slieve Loughshannagh.

Slieve Meelbeg (sliabh maol beag = little bald mountain)
Follow the Mourne Wall down to a sandy gap, then climb uphill over boulders, grass and heather. A cairn marks the summit of Slieve Meelbeg.

Slieve Meelmore (sliabh maol mór = big bald mountain)
The Mourne Wall heads down to a gap, then up a bouldery slope and over a low rise of heathery ground. Another bouldery slope leads to the top of the mountain. A cairn marks the highest point, but it's as well to continue to a sudden dog-leg turn in the wall, where a prominent tower has been built. There is shelter on offer inside the tower.

Slieve Bearnagh (sliabh bearna = mountain of the pass)
The Mourne Wall is followed down a bouldery slope to reach a gap. A steep climb over worn slabs needs care, then the wall leads more easily uphill. The top of Slieve Bearnagh is composed of rocky tors of granite, requiring the use of hands to gain the summit peak.

Slieve Commedagh (sliabh coimheada = mountain of watching)
Continue from Slieve Bearnagh, over the impressive North Tor, then follow the Mourne Wall down bouldery slopes to reach Hare's Gap at a sheepfold. Take care on the next ascent, where a rockstep has to be crossed. After dealing with this obstacle, a fairly easy climb alongside

Clouds blowing off the rocky summit of Slieve Bearnagh

the wall leads over the minor summit of Slievenaglogh. The way
forwards to Slieve Corragh becomes quite bouldery. A walk along a
narrow crest overlooks a series of pinnacles, then a final pull leads to the
broad, grassy top of Slieve Commedagh. There is a tower built into the
wall, providing shelter, but this isn't the highest point on the mountain.
Walk a short way north-west up a gentle slope of short grass to reach
the summit cairn.

Slieve Donard (sliabh Domangard = mountain of Donard)
The Mourne Wall descends from the grassy summit of Slieve
Commedagh, then runs down a heathery slope to reach a gap. A steep,
but fairly easy climb alongside the wall leads to the summit of Slieve
Donard. There is a tower built into the wall, with a trig point perched on
top. A large cairn stands nearby. This is the highest point in both Co
Down and the Province of Ulster. Views can be very extensive, looking
around the Mountains of Mourne, away to the Sperrin Mountains, across
the sea to the Isle of Man and parts of Scotland. In optimum conditions
you could see all the way back to the Wicklow Mountains, where this
guide started. Alas, we're running out of Irish mountains - we've only one
left!

Chimney Rock Mountain

Follow the Mourne Wall down a steep, grassy slope, which becomes bouldery in places, to reach a broad, boggy gap. Walk south-westwards, away from the wall, to cross unmarked slopes leading to Chimney Rock Mountain. Only vague paths lead across heather and stony patches, but the summit is marked with a cairn.

Retrace steps to the Mourne Wall, turn left and follow it across the flanks of Rocky Mountain. The wall turns suddenly right on Long Seefin and runs down towards the Annalong River. The end of the walk is in your hands - according to how much time and energy you have in reserve. Either turn left along a track to reach a minor road, then turn right to follow the road back to Corrigan Bridge, or end the walk by climbing Slieve Binnian, following the Mourne Wall as described in Walk 69.

Alternatives:

There are so many alternative routes over these summits. Slieve Muck, the first mountain of the walk, could be climbed fairly quickly by following a wall uphill from near the Spelga Dam. It's possible to continue along the Mourne Wall to reach Hare's Gap, then follow the Brandy Pad downhill before returning to Spelga Dam via the waymarked Ulster Way. The Brandy Pad can also be followed as part of a walk over the highest summits in the Mountains of Mourne. Slieve Donard is often climbed purely for its own sake. The usual route is from Newcastle, following the Glen River up to the Mourne Wall. An approach can also be made by following a path up from Bloody Bridge.

MOUNTAINS OF IRELAND LISTED BY HEIGHT

MOUNTAINS ABOVE 3,000 FEET

1	Carrauntoohil	3,414
2	Beenkeragh	3,314
3	Caher	3,284
4	Cnoc na Péiste	3,240
5	Caher West Top	3,200
6	Maolán Buí	3,190
7	Cnoc an Chuillin	3,141
8	Brandon Mountain	3,127
9	The Big Gun	3,080
10	Cruach Mhór	3,062
11	Lugnaquillia	3,039
12	Galtymore	3,018

MOUNTAINS BETWEEN 2,000 AND 3,000 FEET

1	Baurtregaum	2,796
2	Slieve Donard	2,796
3	Skregmore East Top	2,792
4	Skregmore	2,790
5	Mullaghcleevaun	2,788
6	Knockbrinnea	2,782
7	Cnoc na Toinne	2,776
8	Brandon Peak	2,764

9	Mangerton Mountain	2,756
10	Purple Mountain	2,739
11	Beenoskee	2,713
12	Caherconree	2,713
13	Lyracappul	2,712
14	Mweelrea	2,688
15	Tonelagee	2,686
16	Nephin	2,646
17	Greenane	2,639
18	Stradbally Mountain	2,627
19	Clohernagh	2,623
20	Ben Lugmore	2,616
21	Mullaghcleevaun East Top	2,615
22	Ben Bury	2,610
23	Mount Leinster	2,610
24	Knockmealdown	2,609
25	Galtybeg	2,600
26	Fauscoum	2,597
27	Temple Hill	2,579
28	Stumpa Duloigh	2,527
29	Mangerton North Top	2,570
30	Coomacarrea	2,541
31	Mullaghanattin	2,539
32	Corrigasleggaun	2,534
33	Knockmoylan	2,521

34	Slieve Commedagh	2,512
35	Croagh Patrick	2,510
36	Masatiompan	2,509
37	Sheefry Hills	2,504
38	Shehy Mountain	2,503
39	Slievemaan	2,501
40	Fauscoum North Top	2,500
41	O'Loughnan's Castle	2,500
42	Sheefry Hills West Top	2,500
43	Camenabologue	2,495
44	Tomies South Top	2,480
45	Knockanaffrin	2,478
46	Kippure	2,475
47	Beann	2,470
48	Errigal	2,466
49	Skregmore West Top	2,450
50	Slieve Binnian	2,449
51	Coumalocha	2,444
52	Teermoyle Mountain	2,442
53	Broaghnabinnia	2,440
54	Sheefry Hills East Top	2,429
55	Conavalla	2,421
56	Tomies Mountain	2,413
57	Blackstairs Mountain	2,409
58	Cnoc an Bhráca	2,398

59	Slieve Cor	2,396
60	Benbaun	2,395
61	Slieve Bearnagh	2,394
62	Seefin	2,387
63	Djouce Mountain	2,385
64	Slievenamon	2,368
65	Duff Hill	2,364
66	Seefingan	2,364
67	Gravale	2,352
68	Meenteog	2,350
69	Corranabinnia	2,343
70	Bencorr	2,336
71	Knockboy	2,321
72	Moanbane	2,313
73	Slieve Meelbeg	2,310
74	Binn idir an Dá Log	2,307
75	Slievelamagan	2,306
76	Ben Gorm	2,303
77	Table Mountain	2,302
78	Camaderry	2,296
79	Silsean	2,296
80	Birreencorragh	2,295
81	Bencollaghduff	2,290
82	Knockaterriff	2,287
83	The Paps (East)	2,284

84	Ben Creggan	2,283
85	Stoompa	2,281
86	Caoinkeen	2,280
87	Keeper Hill	2,279
88	Benbreen	2,276
89	Beann North Top	2,273
90	The Paps (West)	2,273
91	Knocknadobar	2,267
92	Hungry Hill	2,251
93	War Hill	2,250
94	Knockmoyle	2,245
95	Carrigvore	2,244
96	Sawel Mountain	2,240
97	Slieve Snaght	2,240
98	Caherbarnagh	2,239
99	Maumtrasna	2,239
100	Colly	2,238
101	Slieve Meelmore	2,237
102	Turlough Hill	2,228
103	The Back Castles	2,222
104	Derryclare	2,220
105	Knocknagantee	2,220
106	Bluestack	2,219
107	Coomcallee West Top	2,218
108	Lavagh More	2,211

109	Slievemore	2,204
110	Ben Creggan South Top	2,200
111	Corranabinnia South Top	2,200
112	Croaghaun	2,200
113	Slievanea North Top	2,200
114	Beenmore	2,199
115	Knocknafallia	2,199
116	Slieve Muck	2,198
117	Muckish	2,197
118	Letterbreckaun	2,193
119	Cuilcagh	2,188
120	Coomura	2,185
121	Finnararagh	2,185
122	Bengower	2,184
123	Mullaghnarakill	2,182
124	Croaghanmoira	2,181
125	Knocksheegowna	2,181
126	Mullacor	2,179
127	Camenabologue East Top	2,175
128	Stumpa West Top	2,175
129	Binn Mhór	2,174
130	Knockowen	2,169
131	Crohane	2,162
132	Beann West Top	2,155
133	Lugduff	2,154

134	Knockshannahullion	2,153
135	Muckanaght	2,153
136	Chimney Rock Mountain	2,152
137	Knocknagnauv	2,152
138	Ballineddan Mountain	2,151
139	Cnoc na dTarbh	2,150
140	Cove Mountain	2,147
141	Dooish	2,147
142	Keadeen Mountain	2,146
143	Sugarloaf Hill	2,144
144	Dromderalough	2,139
145	Coomcallee	2,135
146	Gowlanebeg	2,134
147	Mullaghanish	2,133
148	Devilsmother	2,131
149	Seahan	2,131
150	Been Hill	2,130
151	Truskmore	2,120
152	Ardnageer	2,118
153	Musheramore	2,118
154	Coomnadiha	2,116
155	Binnia	2,109
156	Scarr	2,108
157	Tonduff	2,107
158	Drung Hill	2,104

159	Beann South Top	2,100
160	Croaghbann	2,100
161	Lavagh Beg	2,100
162	Barrerneen	2,099
163	Knocklomena	2,097
164	Lobawn	2,097
165	Banoge North	2,094
166	Knocknacappul	2,091
167	Mullaghclogha	2,088
168	Knocknadobar East Top	2,087
169	Coomanassig	2,086
170	Bencullagh	2,084
171	Eagle Mountain	2,084
172	Binn Chaonaigh	2,076
173	White Hill	2,075
174	Mullaghaneany	2,070
175	Knockaunabulloga	2,069
176	Glennamong	2,067
177	Benfree	2,065
178	Boughil	2,065
179	Nephin Beg	2,065
180	Meenard Mountain	2,061
181	Shanlieve	2,056
182	Leenaun Hill	2,052
183	Ballysitteragh	2,050

184	Mullach Glas	2,045
185	Maulin	2,044
186	Seefin	2,043
187	Dart Mountain	2,040
188	Corrig Mountain	2,035
189	Slieve Loughshannagh	2,030
190	Slievanea	2,026
191	Slieve Snaght	2,019
192	Coumbaun	2,017
193	Corcogemore	2,012
194	Laghtshanaquilla	2,010
195	Tievebaun	2,007
196	Knockbrack	2,005
197	Coumaraglinmountain	2,000
198	Gullaba Hill	2,000
199	Knocknadobar Far East Top	2,000
200	Monabrack	2,000

This cannot pretend to be a strict "league table" as some heights aren't accurately known. However, it will suffice until the whole of Ireland has been resurveyed and more accurate metric heights become available. I've kept the 3,000-foot summits separate from the rest as there is a considerable gap between those twelve and the other 200. I know of no other list of summits which features such a gap - maybe there's an Irish myth or legend to explain it!

PRINTED BY CARNMOR PRINT & DESIGN
95/97 LONDON ROAD, PRESTON, LANCASHIRE